Edwin Othello Excell

Excellent songs for the church and the Sunday school

Edwin Othello Excell

Excellent songs for the church and the Sunday school

ISBN/EAN: 9783337264994

Printed in Europe, USA, Canada, Australia, Japan

Cover: Foto ©Thomas Meinert / pixelio.de

More available books at **www.hansebooks.com**

EXCELLENT SONGS

FOR THE CHURCH AND THE SUNDAY SCHOOL

EDITED AND PUBLISHED BY

E. O. EXCELL

CHICAGO.

PRICE.
BOARD COVERS.
WORDS AND MUSIC
BY MAIL 25¢ EACH.
BY EXPRESS } $2.50 PER DOZ.
NOT PAID
$20.00 PER 100.

PRICE. LINEN COVERS.
WORDS AND MUSIC
BY MAIL 20¢ EACH
BY EXPRESS } $2.00 PER DOZ.
NOT PAID
$15.00 PER 100.

...Manifesto...

✦ ✦ ✦ ✦ ✦ ✦

As a Singing Evangelist and Musical Director with, over twenty years experience, conducting singing at many of the largest Conventions (International, State and County) ever assembled, I have learned that in order to obtain good, enthusiastic, soul-stirring congregational singing, it is essential to have a liberal supply of song books in the hands of the audience. If the regular Church Hymnal or Sunday School Song Book is used, it is too expensive. To overcome this objection, and that every person who desires to do so may sing, and thereby take part in the service, I have edited "Excellent Songs" for the Church and Sunday School, selecting only the best and most popular copyrights from various books. The binding is neat and substantial, the price within the reach of all.

Hoping that you will profit by my experience and by what I have done.

I am yours truly,

E. O. EXCELL,

The editor and publisher.

Chicago,
Feb. 1st, 1898

MEREDITH, MUSIC PRINTER,

...Excellent Songs...

✦ ✦ ✦ ✦ ✦ ✦ ✦

No. 1.   All Hail the Power.

PERRONET.   CORONATION. C. M.   OLIVER HOLDEN.

1. All hail the pow'r of   Je-sus' name, Let an-gels prostrate fall;
2. Let ev - 'ry kin-dred,   ev - 'ry tribe, On this ter - res-trial ball,
3. Oh, that with yon-der sacred throng We at His feet may fall;

Bring forth the roy - al   di - a - dem, And crown Him Lord of   all;
To Him all maj - es - ty as-cribe, And crown Him Lord of   all;
We'll join the ev - er - last-ing song, And crown Him Lord of   all;

Bring forth the roy - al   di - a - dem, And crown Him Lord   of all.
To Him all maj - es - ty as-cribe, And crown Him Lord   of all.
We'll join the ev - er - last-ing song, And crown Him Lord   of all.

No. 2. The Wonderful Story.

C. H. G.

CHAS. H. GABRIEL.

1. O sweet is the sto-ry of Je-sus, The won-der-ful Savior of
2. He came from the brightest of glo-ry; His blood as a ran-som He
3. His mer-cy flows on like a riv-er, His love is unmeasured and

men, Who suffered and died for the sin-ner—I'll tell it a-
gave, To pur-chase e-ter-nal re-demp-tion, And oh, He is
free; His grace is for-ev-er suf-fi-cient, It reach-es and

CHORUS.

gain and a-gain! } O won - der-ful, wonderful sto - ry, The
might-y to save! } O wonderful sto - - ry, O wonderful story, The
pu-ri-fies me.

dear - est that ever was told...... I'll repeat it in glo - ry, The
dearest that ev - er, that ev-er was told; I'll repeat it in

rit.

wonderful sto - ry, Where I......shall His beauty behold.....
glory, The wonderful story, Where I shall His beau-ty, His beauty behold.

No. 3.   His Love Can Never Fail.

E. S. HALL.　　　　　　　　　　　　　　　　　　　E. O. EXCELL.

1. I do not ask to see the way My feet will have to tread,
2. And if my feet would go a-stray, They can-not, for I know,
3. I will not fear tho' dark-ness come A-broad o'er all the land,

But on - ly that my soul may feed Up - on the liv - ing bread.
That Je- sus guides my falt'ring steps, As joy - ful - ly I go.
If I may on - ly feel the touch Of His own lov - ing hand.

'Tis bet - ter far that I should walk By faith close to His side,
And tho' I may not see His face, My faith is strong and clear,
And tho' I trem - ble when I think How weak I am, how frail,

FINE.

I may not know the way I go, But Oh, I know my Guide.
That in each hour of sore dis-tress My Sav - ior will be near.
My soul is sat - is - fied to know His love can nev-er fail.

D. S.—*My soul is sat - is-fied to know, His love can nev-er fail.*

CHORUS.　　　　　　　　　　　　　　　　　　　　D. S.

His love.... can nev-er fail, His love.... can nev-er fail.
His love can nev - er fail,　　　His love can nev- er fail.

No. 4.   Young Peoples Army.

CHARLOTTE G. HOMER. Copyright, 1895, by Chas. H. Gabriel.   Mrs. CARRIE B. ADAMS.

Cho.-1. March a-long to-geth-er firm and true, For lo, the world is
2. On we go with ar-mor shin-ing bright, With sword in hand to
3. True as steel and loy-al to our King, We'll fight un-til the

ev-er watching you; Be brave and bold up-on the bat-tle
bat-tle for the right; U-nit-ed in the serv-ice of the
shouts of vic-t'ry ring From North, from South, from East, and from the

FINE.   UNISON SOLO.

field, De-termined that the foe shall yield. Long and loud the
Lord We're marching at our Cap-tain's word. Val-iant sol-diers
West, And Christ is ev-'ry-where con-fess'd. Storm the forts of

bu-gle call is sound-ing! Sin and wrong are ev'ry-where abounding,
of the Lord are lead-ing, Ear-nest-ly for help the church is pleading,
sin and des-o-la-tion; Soldiers brave, renew your ob-li-ga-tion;

D. C. Cho.

"Forward" all a-long the line resounding, Bids us march a-way.
Slow-ly backward see the foe re-ced-ing, Forward march to-day.
And with earnest pray'r and supplication Forward march to-day.

No. 5.   Open the Door for the Children.

U. N. O.   E. O. EXCELL.

1. O-pen the door for the chil-dren, Ten-der-ly gath-er them in;
2. O-pen the door for the chil-dren, See, they are com-ing in throngs;
3. O-pen the door for the chil-dren, Take the dear lambs by the hand,

In from the high-way and hedges, In from the plac-es of sin;
Bid them sit down to the ban-quet, Teach them your beautiful songs,
Point them to truth and to goodness, Lead them to Canaan's fair land,

Some are so young and so help-less, Some are so hun-gry and cold;
Pray you the Fa-ther to bless them, Pray you that grace may be given;
Some are so young and so help-less, Some are so hun-gry and cold;

FINE.

O - pen the door for the chil-dren, Gath-er them in-to the fold.
O - pen the door for the chil-dren, Theirs is the kingdom of heaven.
O - pen the door for the chil-dren, Gath-er them in-to the fold.

D. S.—*O-pen the door for the chil-dren, Gath-er them in-to the fold.*

CHORUS.   D.S.

O - - pen the door, . . .   Gath - er them in, ...
O - pen the door, o - pen the door, Gath-er them in, gath-er them in.

No. 6. Let the Sunshine in.

ADA BLENKHORN. COPYRIGHT, 1895, BY CHAS. H. GABRIEL. CHAS. H. GABRIEL.

1. Do you fear the foe will in the con-flict win? Is it
2. Does your faith grow fainter in the cause you love? Are your
3. Would you go re-joic-ing on the up-ward way, Know-ing

dark with-out you,—dark-er still with-in? Clear the darkened
pray'rs un-ans-wer'd by your God a-bove? Clear the darkened
naught of darkness,—dwelling in the day? Clear the darkened

windows, o-pen wide the door, Let a lit-tle sun-shine in.
windows, o-pen wide the door, Let a lit-tle sun-shine in.
windows, o-pen wide the door, Let a lit-tle sun-shine in.

CHORUS.

Let a lit-tle sun-shine in . . . Let a lit-tle sunshine in; . .
the sunshine in, the sunshine in,

Clear the darkened windows, open wide the door, Let a little sunshine in.

No. 7. Never Lose Sight of Jesus.

Rev. J. OATMAN JR.

E. O. EXCELL.

1. O Pilgrim bound for the heav'nly land, Nev-er lose sight of Je - sus;
2. When e'er you're tempted to go a-stray, Nev-er lose sight of Je - sus;
3. Tho' dark the pathway may seem ahead, Nev-er lose sight of Je - sus;
4. When death is knocking outside the door, Nev-er lose sight of Je - sus;

He'll lead you gen-tly with lov-ing hand, Nev-er lose sight of Je - sus.
Press on-ward, upward the nar-row way, Nev-er lose sight of Je - sus.
"I will be with you" His word hath said, Nev-er lose sight of Je - sus.
Till safe-ly land-ed on Canaan's shore, Nev-er lose sight of Je - sus.

CHORUS.

Nev - er lose sight of Je - sus, Nev - er lose sight of Je - sus;

Day and night He will lead you right, Nev - er lose sight of Je - sus.

No. 8. Jesus is Calling.

F. S. S. COPYRIGHT, 1898, BY E. O. EXCELL. F. S. SHEPARD.

1. Je - sus, the Sav - ior, is call - ing for thee, "Come heav - y -
2. Ye who are wan-der-ing now far a - way, Heed the blest
3. Je - sus still seeks thee a - far from the fold, Out on the

la - den one, come un - to me; I will thy soul from its
mes - sage—why long-er de - lay? Why from His pres-ence so
mount-ain so dark and so cold; Turn to Him now—in His

bur - dens set free"— Je - sus is call - ing for thee!
long wilt thou stay? Je - sus is call - ing for thee!
arms He'll en - fold— Je - sus is call - ing for thee!

REFRAIN.

Je-sus is call - ing, Ten-der-ly call - ing, Je-sus is
call-ing for thee, call-ing for thee,

call-ing, calling for thee; Je-sus is call-ing, call-ing for thee.

No. 9. For the Sake of Jesus.

ADA BLENKHORN.

E. O. EXCELL.

1. There's a world from sin to save, For the sake of Je - sus;
2. There are cheer-ful words to speak, For the sake of Je - sus;
3. There are foes that we must fight, For the sake of Je - sus;

There are dan - gers great to brave, For the sake of Je - sus.
There are wand'ring souls to seek, For the sake of Je - sus.
There are wrongs that we must right, For the sake of Je - sus.

As the world we jour - ney thro', With the cross and crown in view,
There are hun-gry ones to feed, There are falt'ring steps to lead,
Ere the set - ting of the sun, Ere the work of life is done,

:S: FINE.

There's so much that we can do, For the sake of Je - sus.
Let us do each lov - ing deed, For the sake of Je - sus.
There are king-doms to be won, For the sake of Je - sus.

D. S.—*There's so much that we can do, For the sake of Je - sus.*

REFRAIN. D. S.

For the sake of Je - sus, For the sake of Je - sus;

No. 10. There is Glory in My Soul.

Mrs. GRACE WEISER DAVIS. Copyright, 1894, by Chas. H. Gabriel.   CHAS. H. GABRIEL.

1. Since I lost my sins, and I found my Sav-ior, There is
2. Since He cleansed my heart, gave me sight for blindness, There is
3. Since with God I've walked, hav-ing sweet com-mun-ion, There is
4. Since I en-tered Canaan on my way to heav-en, There is

glo-ry in my soul! Since by faith I sought and obtained God's favor,
glo-ry in my soul! Since He touch'd and heal'd me in loving kindness,
glo-ry in my soul! Brighter grows each day in this heav'nly un-ion,
glo-ry in my soul! Since the day my life to the Lord was giv-en,

CHORUS.

There is glo-ry in my soul. Yes, there's glory, glory, there is glory in my soul!

glo-ry, glo-ry,

Ev-'ry day bright-er grows, And I con-quer all my foes; There is

glo-ry, glo-ry, yes, there's glory in my soul, There is glory in my soul!

glo-ry, glo-ry,   glory in my soul.

No. 11. Scatter Sunshine.

LANTA WILSON SMITH. COPYRIGHT, 1892, BY E. O. EXCELL. E. O. EXCELL.

1. In a world where sorrow Ev - er will be known, Where are found the
2. Slight-est ac-tions oft - en Meet the sor-est needs, For the world wants
3. When the days are gloomy, Sing some happy song, Meet the world's re-

need - y, And the sad and lone; How much joy and com-fort
dai - ly, Lit - tle kind - ly deeds; Oh, what care and sor-row,
pin - ing, With a cour - age strong; Go with faith un-daunt-ed,

You can all be-stow, If you scat-ter sunshine Ev-'ry-where you go.
You may help remove, With your songs and courage, Sympathy and love.
Thro' the ills of life, Scatter smiles and sunshine, O'er its toil and strife,

CHORUS.

Scat - ter sun-shine all a-long your way, Cheer and bless and
Scatter the smiles and   o-ver the way,

1. 2.

brighten Ev - 'ry pass-ing day, Ev - 'ry pass-ing day.

No. 12.　　Glory! Jesus Saves.

F. M. D

FRANK M. DAVIS.

1. { I have bathed in the fount for the cleansing of sin,　Glo - ry,
   { I have found sweet re-lief and a joy　with - in,　Glo - ry,

2. { I am ful - ly redeem'd by the blood of the lamb,　Glo - ry,
   { I will wit - ness for Je - sus wher - ev - er I am;　Glo - ry,

3. { At the cross of my Sav - ior I first found the light, Glo - ry,
   { I was blind but 'twas there I re-ceived my sight;　Glo - ry,

glo - ry, Je - sus saves; }
glo - ry, Je - sus 　　　 } saves; Oh, that won-der - ful fount-ain of
glo - ry, Je - sus saves; }
glo - ry, Je - sus 　　　 } saves; By His won-der - ful grace and His
glo - ry, Je - sus saves, }
glo - ry, Je - sus 　　　 } saves; I re - joice that by faith I in

mer - cy free, Flow - ing so sweet-ly from Cal-va - ry, Now the
pow'r di - vine, Je-sus has chang'd this poor heart of mine, Now with
Him a - bide, Je - sus, my Lord, the once cru-ci - fied, With His

soul cleansing pow'r reaches e-ven me, Glo-ry, glo-ry, Je - sus saves.
joy I can say I am whol-ly Thine, Glo-ry, glo-ry, Je - sus saves.
peace in my soul I am sat-is - fied, Glo-ry, glo-ry, Je - sus saves.

No. 13.   There's Much We Can Do.

Mrs. E. C. ELLSWORTH.   COPYRIGHT, 1885, BY E. O. EXCELL.   E. O. EXCELL.

1. There's much we can do if we work with a will, No
   The Mas - ter is read - y our la - bors to bless, And
2. So much we can do in the sow - ing of seed, Some
   The foe will be bus - y in spread - ing the tares, Then
3. So much we can do in the reap - ing of wheat, Some
   So much may be lost when the har - vest is past, If

1.
time to be wast - ed to - day;
(omit.)
fields are yet bar - ren and waste,
(omit.)
fields for the har-vest are white;
(omit.)

2.
wag - es he of - fers to pay.
go, and be work-ing with haste.
left to the mil-dew and blight.

CHORUS.

No time to be wast - ed for man - y the fields, And
la - borers, as ev - er, are few;
as ev - er are few;
A - way to the
work that is needing a hand! *So much! O so much we can do!*

No. 14. He Hideth Me.

ADA BLENKHORN. CHAS. H. GABRIEL.

1. He hid - eth me when storms are near, In the shel - ter of
2. He hid - eth me from ev - 'ry foe, In the shel - ter of
3. He hid - eth me when - e'er I fear, In the shel - ter of
4. He hid - eth me what - e'er be - tides, In the shel - ter of

His wounded side; Se - cure from ev - 'ry doubt and fear, In the
His wounded side; He gives me joy for all my woe, In the
His wounded side; He com-forts me with words of cheer, In the
His wounded side; With - in my soul His peace a - bides, In the

CHORUS.

shel - ter of His wounded side.
shel - ter of His wounded side.
shel - ter of His wounded side.
shel - ter of His wounded side.

Hid - ing, safe - ly
Hid-ing, safe-ly hid-ing, I am

hid - ing, In the shel - ter of His wound - ed
hid - ing, safe - ly hid - ing

side; I am hid - ing, (I am) shel - ter of His wound - ed side.

No. 15. All the World for Christ.

S. WOLCOTT.   E. O. EXCELL.

1. "Christ for the world," we sing; The world to Christ we bring With love and
2. "Christ for the world," we sing; The world to Christ we bring With fer-vent
3. "Christ for the world," we sing; The world to Christ we bring With one ac-
4. "Christ for the world," we sing; The world to Christ we bring With joy-ful

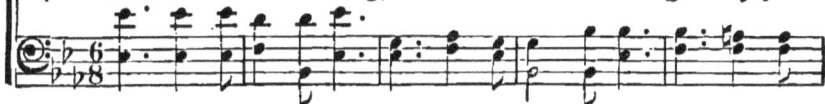

zeal; The poor, and them that mourn, The faint and o - ver-borne,
prayer; The way-ward and the lost, By rest-less pas-sion toss'd,
cord; With us the work to share, With us reproach to dare,
song; The new-born souls, whose days, Reclaim'd from er-rors' ways,

CHORUS.

Sin-sick and sorrow-worn, Whom Christ doth heal.
Redeemed, at countless cost, From dire de-spair. } All, all for Christ,
With us the cross to bear For Christ, our Lord. } All, all, all for Christ,
Inspired with hope and praise, To Christ be-long.

All, all for Him,   All, all the world for Christ, All, all for Him.
All,   all,   all for Him,

No. 16.   The Cross is not Greater.

B. B.

Commander
BALLINGTON BOOTH.

DUET.

1. The cross that He gave may be heavy, But it ne'er outweighs His grace;
2. The thornes in my path are not sharper Than composed His crown for me;
3. The scorn of my foes may be dar-ing, For they bow'd and mock'd my God;
4. The light of His love shines the brighter, As it falls on paths of woe;
5. His will I have joy in ful-fill-ing As I'm walking in His sight,

The storm that I fear'd may surround me, But it ne'er ex-cludes His face.
The cup which I drink not more bitter Than He drank in Gethsem-a-ne.
They'll hate me for ho-ly liv-ing, For they cru-ci-fied my Lord.
The toil of my work grows lighter As I stoop to raise the low.
My all to the blood I am bringing, It a-lone can keep me right.

CHORUS.

The cross is not great-er than His grace,
The storm can-not hide his blessed face;

than His grace.
bless-ed face,

} I am sat-is-fied to

know That with Je-sus here be-low I can con-quer ev-'ry foe.

conquer ev-'ry foe, ev-'ry foe.

No. 17. Walk in the Light.

ISAAC WATTS.   COPYRIGHT, 1887, BY E. O. EXCELL.   E. O. EXCELL.

1. Am I   a sol-dier of the cross,   A   fol - low'r of the Lamb?
2. Must I   be carried to the skies   On   flow-ery beds of ease?
3. Are there   no foes for me to face?   Must I   not stem the flood?
4. Sure I   must fight, if I would reign;   In-crease my courage, Lord;

And shall I fear to own his cause   Or blush to speak his name?
While oth-ers fought to win the prize,   And sailed thro' bloody seas?
Is this vile world a friend to grace,   To help me on to God?
I'll bear the toil, en-dure the pain,   Sup - port - ed by thy word.

CHORUS.

Let us walk   in the   Light,...... Let us   walk   in the
Let us walk   in the Light,   Let us walk

Light..........   Oh, let us   walk   in   the
in the Light,   Oh, let   us   walk

Light,.........   In the Light, the beau - ti - ful light of God.
In the Light,

No. 18. I Never Will Cease to Love Him.

C. H. G.   COPYRIGHT, 1894, BY E. O. EXCELL.   CHAS. H. GABRIEL.

1. For all the Lord has done for me, I nev-er will cease to love Him;
2. He gives me strength for ev'ry day, I nev-er will cease to love Him;
3. Tho' all the world His love neglect, I nev-er will cease to love Him;
4. He saves me ev - 'ry day and hour, I nev-er will cease to love Him;
5. While on my journey here be-low, I nev-er will cease to love Him;

And for His grace so rich and free, I nev-er will cease to love Him.
He leads and guides me all the way, I nev-er will cease to love Him.
I could not such a Friend re-ject I nev-er will cease to love Him.
Just now I feel His cleansing pow'r, I nev-er will cease to love Him.
And when to that bright world I go, I nev-er will cease to love Him.

CHORUS.

I nev-er will cease to love Him, my Sav-ior, my Sav - ior;
I nev-er will cease to love Him, He's my Sav-ior, He's my Sav - ior;

I nev-er will cease to love Him, He's done so much for me.
I nev-er will cease to love Him, For He's done so much for me,

No. 19. Since I Have Been Redeemed.

E. O. E.   COPYRIGHT, 1884, BY E. O. EXCELL.   E. O. EXCELL.

1. I have a *song* I love to sing, Since I have been re-deem'd,
2. I have a *Christ* that sat-is-fies, Since I have been re-deem'd,
3. I have a *Wit-ness* bright and clear, Since I have been re-deem'd,
4. I have a *joy* I can't ex-press, Since I have been re-deem'd,
5. I have a *home* pre-pared for me, Since I have been re-deem'd,

Of my Re-deem-er, Sav-ior, King, Since I have been re-deem'd.
To do His will my high-est prize, Since I have been re-deem'd.
Dis-pell-ing ev-'ry doubt and fear, Since I have been re-deem'd.
All thro' His blood and right-eous-ness, Since I have been re-deem'd.
Where I shall dwell e-ter-nal-ly, Since I have been re-deem'd.

CHORUS.

Since I . . . . . . have been re-deem'd,   Since I have been redeem'd,
Since I have been redeem'd, Since I have been redeem'd,

I will glo-ry in His name, I will glo-ry in my Sav-ior's name.

No. 20.　More Like Jesus.

J. M. S.

COPYRIGHT, 1878, BY J. M. STILLMAN.
COPYRIGHT, 1898, BY E. O. EXCELL.

J. M. STILLMAN. Mus. Doo.

1. I want to be more like Je - sus, And fol-low Him day　by　day;
2. I want to be kind and gen-tle, To those who are in　dis-tress;
3. I want to be meek and low-ly, Like Je - sus, our Friend and King;
4. I want to be pure and ho - ly, As pure as the crys - tal snow;

I want to be true and faith-ful, And ev - 'ry command o-bey.
To com-fort the brok-en heart-ed, With sweet words of ten-der-ness.
I want to be strong and ear-nest, And souls to the Sav-ior bring.
I want to love Je - sus dear - ly, For Je-sus loves me, I know.

REFRAIN.

More and more like Je - sus,　I would ev - er　be, ...
I . . . . ,　ev-er would be,

More and more like Je - sus, My Sav-ior who died for　me.

No. 21. The Bible.

BARTON. COPYRIGHT, 1887, BY E. O. EXCELL. E. O. EXCELL.

1. Lamp of our feet, where-by we trace Our path when apt to stray;
2. Bread of our souls, where-on we feed; True man - na from on high;
3. Word of the Ev - er - last-ing God, Will of His glo-rious Son;
4. Lord, grant us all a - right to learn The wis-dom it im - parts,

Stream from the fount of heav'nly grace, Brook, by the trav-'ler's way.
Our guide and chart, wherein we read Of realms be-yond the sky.
With-out Thee how could earth be trod, Or heav'n it - self be won?
And to its heav'n-ly teach-ing turn With sim - ple child-like hearts.

CHORUS.

Beau - ti-ful Lamp, bright-ly shine . . . on the way, ...
Beau-ti-ful Lamp, Beau-ti-ful Lamp, Shine on the way, Shine on the way,

Rit.

Guid - ing the soul . . . . to the man - sions of day. . . . .
Guid-ing the soul, guid-ing the soul to the mansions of day, to the mansions of day.

No. 22.   I Shall Be Satisfied.

Rev. G. W. CROFTS.   WORDS AND MUSIC.   CHAS. H. GABRIEL.

1. I shall be sat - is - fied at last   On heav'n's e - ter - nal shore,
2. I shall be sat - is - fied when sin   Has all been wash'd a - way,
3. I shall be sat - is - fied when love, My por - tion blest shall be,
4. I shall be sat - is - fied when I   No more shall leave His side;

When all the storms of life are past, That now a-round me roar.
When ho - li- ness shall reign with-in, Pure as the per-fect day.
When peace, like a ce - les-tial dove, Shall spread its wings o'er me.
When God shall wake me with a smile   I shall be sat - is - fied.

CHORUS.

. I........shall be sat - is-fied, Satisfied when Je - sus takes me,
I shall be satisfied, satisfied at last,

I........shall be sat - is-fied, Sat - is- fied when God a-wakes me,
I shall be satisfied, satisfied at last,

No. 23. Let Him In.

Rev. J. B. ATCHINSON. E. O. EXCELL.

1. There's a strang-er at the door, Let Him in;
2. O - pen now to Him your heart, Let Him in;
3. Hear you now His lov-ing voice? Let Him in;
4. Now ad - mit the heavenly Guest, Let Him in;

Let the Savior in, let the Savior in;

He has been there oft be - fore, Let Him in;
If you wait He will de - part, Let Him in;
Now, oh, now make Him your choice, Let Him in;
He will make for you a feast, Let Him in;

Let the Savior in, let the Savior in;

Let Him in, ere He is gone, Let Him in, the Ho - ly One,
Let Him in, He is your Friend, He your soul will sure de - fend,
He is stand-ing at the door, Joy to you He will re - store,
He will speak your sins for-given, And when earth ties all are riven,

Je-sus Christ, the Fa-ther's Son, Let Him in.
He will keep you to the end, Let Him in.
And His name you will a - dore, Let Him in.
He will take you home to heaven, Let Him in.

Let the Savior in, let the Savior in.

No. 24. Look and Live.

W. A. O.   W. A. OGDEN.

1. I've a mes-sage from the Lord, Hal - le - lu - jah! The
2. I've a mes-sage full of love, Hal - le - lu - jah! A
3. Life is of - fered un - to thee, Hal - le - lu - jah! E -
4. I will tell you how I came; Hal - le - lu - jah! To

mes-sage un - to you I'll give, 'Tis re - cord-ed in His word,
mes-sage, oh! my friend for you, 'Tis a mes-sage from a - bove,
ter - nal life thy soul shall have, If you'll on - ly look to Him,
Je - sus, when He made me whole; 'Twas be - liev-ing on His name,

D. S. *'Tis re - cord - ed in His word,*

FINE.

Hal - le - lu - jah! It is on - ly that you "look and live."
Hal - le - lu - jah! Je - sus said it; and I know 'tis true.
Hal - le - lu - jah! Look to Je - sus, who a - lone can save.
Hal - le - lu - jah! I trust - ed and He saved my soul.

Hal - le - lu - jah! It is on - ly that you "look and live."

CHORUS. D. S.

"Look and live," my brother, live, Look to Je-sus now and live,
"Look and live," my brother, live, "Look and live."

No. 25. God is Calling Yet.

GERHARD TERSTEEGEN.   E. O. EXCELL.

1. God calling yet! shall I not hear? Earth's pleasures shall I still hold dear?
2. God calling yet! shall I not rise? Can I His lov-ing voice de-spise,
3. God calling yet! and shall He knock, And I my heart the closer lock?
4. God calling yet! I can-not stay; My heart I yield with out de-lay;

Shall life's swift passing years all fly, And still my soul in slumber lie?
And base-ly His kind care re-pay? He calls me still; can I de-lay?
He still is wait-ing to re-ceive, And shall I dare His Spirit grieve?
Vain world, fare-well, from thee I part; The voice of God has reach'd my heart.

CHORUS.

Call - - ing, oh, hear Him, Call - ing, oh, hear Him, God is calling
God is call-ing yet,   God is call-ing yet;

yet, oh, hear Him calling, calling, Call - ing, oh, hear Him, Call - -
God is call-ing yet,   God is call-ing

ing, oh, hear Him, God is call-ing yet, oh, hear Him calling yet.
yet,

No. 26. To Please Jesus.

COPYRIGHT, 1898, BY E. O. EXCELL.
WORDS AND MUSIC

C. H. G.   CHAS. H. GABRIEL.

1. I will not go where I can-not take Je-sus, Je-sus my
2. I will not do what I know would grieve Je-sus, How could I
3. I'll not be-lieve what I can-not tell Je-sus, Nor will I
4. I'll do what-ev-er I know will please Je-sus, I will be

Sav-ior, my Friend and Guide, For I should tremble to feel for one
spurn such a Friend as He? No! for a life-time of tenderest de-
think up-on things un-true; For in the light or the dark-ness He
faith-ful in ev-'ry thing; Yes, by the help and the grace that He

CHORUS.

mo-ment That He was ab-sent from my side. Stay with me, Sav-ior,
vo-tion Can-not re-pay His love to me.
sure-ly Know-eth all things we think or do.
gives me, I will be loy-al to my King.

Keep me, I pray; Nev-er a moment let me stray, Help me more oft-en Thy

love to re-mem-ber, That I may live clos-er, clos-er to Thee.

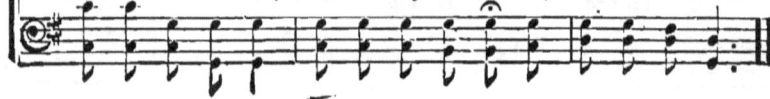

No. 27. All for Jesus.

Rev. J. B. ATCHINSON. COPYRIGHT, 1889 BY E. O. EXCELL. E. O. EXCELL.

1. All, yes all I give to Je - sus, It be-longs to Him,
2. All, yes all I give to Je - sus, It be-longs to Him,
3. All, yes all I give to Je - sus, It be-longs to Him,
4. All, yes all I give to Je - sus, It be-longs to Him,

All my heart I give to Je - sus, It be-longs to Him,
All my voice I give to Je - sus, It be-longs to Him,
All my love I give to Je - sus, It be-longs to Him,
All my life I give to Je - sus, It be-longs to Him,

Ev - er-more to be His dwelling, Ev - er-more His praises swell-ing,
Pleading for the young, and hoary, Tell-ing of His pow'r and glo-ry,
Lov-ing Him for love un-ceas-ing, For His mer-cy e'er in-creas-ing,
Hour by hour I'll live for Je - sus, Day, by day I'll work for Je - sus,

Ev - er-more His good-ness tell-ing, It be-longs to Him.
Sing-ing o'er and o'er the sto - ry, It be-longs to Him.
For His watchcare nev - er ceas-ing, It be-longs to Him.
Ev - er-more I'll hon - or Je - sus, It be-longs to Him.

No. 28. Bless Me Now.

COPYRIGHT, 1897, BY E. O. EXCELL

E. A. H.   WORDS AND MUSIC.   Rev. ELISHA A. HOFFMAN.

1. Je - sus Christ, my lov-ing Sav-ior, Pure and ho - ly   I would be;
2. Could the time be more pro-pi-tious Than this con-se - cra - ted hour,
3. This, O this is my pe-ti-tion: "Cleanse my heart from ev - 'ry stain;"

Look up - on Thy child with fav-or; Make me more and more like Thee;
Or the mo-ment more au-spi-cious For Thy won-der-work-ing power?
This I plead, in deep con-tri-tion: "Lord, let not a sin re-main;"

For Thy love my soul is pin - ing, For Thy per-fect righteousness;
Come, O come while I am bend-ing, Humbly at Thy feet the knee,
Hear and bless me, ten-der Sav - ior! Pure and spot-less I would be;

𝄪

FINE.

Come, dear Lord, with grace re-fin-ing, Per-fect me in ho - li - ness.
Come, O breath of God! descending, Fall in bless-ing up - on me.
Now be-stow Thy grace and fav-or, Now re-fine and cleanse Thou me.

D. C.—*blood a-ton-ing, Make, O make me pure with-in.*

CHORUS.   D. S.

Bless me, bless me, Cleanse me from all sin; Wash me in the
Bless me now, Bless me now,

No. 29. Savior, Wash Me in the Blood.

COWPER.
COPYRIGHT, 1887, BY E. O. EXCELL.
E. O. EXCELL.

1. { There is a fountain fill'd with blood, Drawn from Immanuel's veins; }
{ And sin-ners plung'd beneath that flood, Lose all their guilt-y stains. }

2. { The dy - ing thief re-joiced to see That fount-ain in his day, }
{ And there may I tho' vile as he, Wash all my sins a - way. }

CHORUS.

Sav - ior, wash . . . . . me in the blood, Sav-ior,
Sav - ior, wash me in the blood, In the blood, the blood of the Lamb, Sav - ior,

wash . . . . . me in the blood, Oh, wash . . . .
wash me in the blood, In the blood, the blood of the Lamb, Oh, wash me in the

. . . me in the blood, And I shall be whiter than the snow.
blood, in the blood, the blood of the Lamb,

3 Thou dying Lamb, Thy precious blood
Shall never lose its power,
Till all the ransomed church of God
Are saved, to sin no more.

4 E'er since by faith I saw the stream,
Thy flowing wounds supply,
Redeeming love has been my theme,
And shall be till I die.

No. 30.   Something for Theē.

Wм: H. Gardner.   E. H. Packard.

1. My   tal - ents are few, dear - est Mas - ter,.... Yet I
2. I   can - not with fi - er - y   warn - ings,.. Make the
3. No   rich - es, a - lasl can I give thee... For they

long of some use   to be, Then, tell me,   I pray thee, dear
wick - ed their guilt to see, Yet sure - ly some path ·way is
nev - er have come to me, But free - ly I lay on thy

Je - sus, How may I   do some - thing for thee?
o - pen, Where I   may do some - thing for thee.
al - tar, My life, . to do some - thing for thee.

Refrain.

Some - thing for   thee,...... some - thing for thee,...... Oh,

Something for thee,   something for thee,

tell me, I pray thee, dear Master, How may I do something for thee?

No. 31. He is Able to Deliver Thee.

W. A. O. COPYRIGHT, 1887, BY E. O. EXCELL. W. A. OGDEN.

1. 'Tis the grand-est theme thro' the a - ges rung; 'Tis the
2. 'Tis the grand-est theme in the earth or main; 'Tis the
3. 'Tis the grand-est theme, let the ti - dings roll, To the

grand - est theme for a mor - tal tongue, 'Tis the grand-est theme
grand - est theme for a mor - tal strain, 'Tis the grand-est theme
guilt - y heart, to the sin - ful soul, Look to God in faith,

FINE.

that the world e'er sung, "Our God is a-ble to de - liv - er thee."
tell the world a - gain, "Our God is a-ble to de - liv - er thee."
He will make thee whole, "Our God is a-ble to de - liv - er thee."

D. S.—*Him for rest; "Our God is a-ble to de - liv - er thee."*

CHORUS.

He is a - - - - ble to de - liv - er thee, He is
a - ble, He is a - ble

D. S.

a - - - ble to de - liv - er thee; Tho' by sin op-prest, Go to
a - ble, He is a - ble

No. 32. Ring, Beautiful Bells!

E. A. H.   COPYRIGHT, 1889, BY E. O. EXCELL.   Rev. ELISHA A. HOFFMAN.

1. Ring, ring, beau-ti-ful bells, Peal - ing far and near,   In   the
2. Sing, sing, lit - tle ones sing, On this best of days;   Fill this
3. O   ye beau-ti-ful birds! Fill with song the air;   Mak-ing

valleys and dells, Loud and   clear; Sum-mon to the house of God
beau - ti-ful place With God's   praise; Praise him for his wondrous love
mel - o-dy sweet Ev - 'ry - where; Join us in our grateful lays,

All whose feet may roam a - broad; Ring, ring, beau - ti - ful bells,
For   all bless-ings from a - bove, Sing, sing, lit - tle ones sing
Help us swell the songs of praise, Mak - ing mel - o - dy sweet,

Fine.   *D S.*

Loud and   clear. Ring, ring, ring, ring! Ring, ring, ring, ring!
To God's praise. Sing, sing, sing, sing! Sing, sing, sing sing!
Ev - 'ry - where. Sing, sing, sing, sing! Sing, sing, sing, sing!

No. 33. Blessed Be the Fountain.

W. A. O. COPYRIGHT, 1889, BY E. O. EXCELL. W. A. OGDEN.

1. Blessed be the fountain of life to-day! Flowing free,
2. Many have been cleansed in that fount of sin, Flowing free,
3. Lin-ger not a-way from this fountain pure, Flowing free, Flow-ing free,

flow-ing free, There the soul may wash all its guilt a-way,
flow-ing free, so free, Ma-ny yet, will come, and will wash there-in,
flow-ing free, so free, For the guilt-y soul 'tis a wond'rous cure,

CHORUS.

In that foun-tain of life, flow-ing free! Oh! .... the
Blessed foun-tain of life, flow-ing free! Oh, the blessed fount,
Blessed foun-tain of life, flow-ing free!

blessed foun-tain of life! free-ly flow-ing, To .... that
the bless-ed fount, To that bless-ed fount,

rit. Repeat ad lib.

bless-ed foun-tain, I'll go and I'll wash, and be clean.
the fount of life, be clean.

No. 34. Hark! There's a Call.

Rev E. A. HOFFMAN. COPYRIGHT, 1889, BY E. O. EXCELL. M. L. McPHAIL.

1. Hark! there's a call for the brave and true! Brother, en-list, for the
2. Come to the front, brother, take a stand; Fall in - to line at your
3. Who'll vol-un - teer in the ranks to-day, Read-y to plunge in the

Lord wants you! Fac - ing the foe with your sword in hand,
Lord's com-mand; Fol - low his lead in the ear - nest fight,
thick - est fray? Je - sus now waits for the brave and true;

Brave-ly go forth at your Lord's command. Hear the call,(brother,)
Con - quer for God, and for truth and right.
Broth - er, en-list! for the Lord wants you.

CHORUS.

hear the call, Pleading for help from one and all; Hear the call,

(brother,) hear the call, Plead - ing for help from one and all.

No. 35.   Redeeming Love.

M. MADAN.   COPYRIGHT, 1889, BY E. O. EXCELL.   H. A. LEWIS.

1. Now be-gin the heav'nly theme, Sing a - loud in Je - sus' name;
2. Ye who see the Fa-ther's grace Beaming in the Savior's face,
3. Wel-come all by sin op-pressed, Welcome to his sa - cred rest:

Ye who Je - sus' kindness prove, Tri-umph in re-deem-ing love.
As to Ca - naan on ye move, Praise and bless re-deem-ing love.
Noth-ing bro't him from a - bove, Noth-ing but re-deem-ing love

CHORUS.

Hith-er, then your mu-sic bring,

Hith - er, then......your mu-sic bring,...... Strike a-

Strike a-loud each joyful string; Mortals, join

loud......... each joy - ful string............... Mor-tals join..... ..... the hosts a-

the host a-bove, Join to praise re-deem-ing love.

bove..................... Join to praise............ redeeming love.................

No. 36. Calling the Prodigal.

C. H. G. COPYRIGHT, 1889, BY E. O. EXCELL. CHAS. H. GABRIEL.

1. { God is call-ing the prod-i-gal, come with-out de-lay, Hear, O
   { Tho' you've wander'd so far from His presence, come to-day, Hear His

2. { Pa-tient, lov-ing, and ten-der-ly still the Fa-ther pleads, Hear, O
   { Oh! re-turn while the spir-it in mer-cy in-ter-cedes, Hear His

3. { Come, there's bread in the house of thy Fa-ther, and to spare, Hear, O
   { Lo! the ta-ble is spread and the feast is waiting there, Hear His

hear Him call-ing, call-ing now for thee,
lov-ing voice   (*Omit.*)
                                    for thee,
call-ing still. . . . .
call-ing still.

CHORUS.

Call - - ing now for thee, ... Oh! wea - - ry prodigal,
Calling now for thee,   Calling now for thee,   weary prodigal, come,

come, ... ,   Call - - ing now for thee, ...
wea-ry prod-i-gal, come,   Call-ing now for thee,   call-ing now for thee,

Oh, wea - - - - ry prod-i-gal, come. . . . .
wea-ry prod-i-gal, come,   wea-ry prod-i-gal come.

No. 37. The Great Redeemer Lives.

RICHARD BURNHAM.   HENRY A. LEWIS.

1. Now I know the great Redeemer, Know he lives and spreads his fame;
2. My Re-deem-er lives within me, Lives, and heav'nly life conveys;
3. Par- don, peace, and full sal-va- tion, From my liv-ing Sav-ior flow;

Lives, and all the heav'ns adore him; Lives, and earth resounds his name.
Lives, and glo-ry now surrounds me; Lives, and I his name shall praise.
Light and life, and con-so-la-tion, All the good I e'er can know;

CHORUS.

Soon shall I   be-hold the Sav -ior,
Soon shall I.......... be-hold the Sav   -   ior,   He who

He who lives   ·   and reigns a- bove,   Lives, and I
lives...... and reigns above,........ Lives, and I...... shall live for-

shall live for- ev- er,   Live and sing   re-deem-ing love.
ev   ·   er, Live and sing........ redeeming   love.,......

No. 38. I Love to Sing About Jesus.

LANTA WILSON SMITH.   CHAS. H. GABRIEL.

1. I love to sing a-bout Je - sus, When all are glad and gay;
2. I love to sing a-bout Je - sus, When sor-row clouds the day;
3. I love to sing a-bout Je - sus, It keeps my heart from sin;
4. I love to sing a-bout Je - sus, 'Tis all that I can do;

The heart sings out with a joy-ful shout The words that we long to say.
I know some song of His ten-der love Will scat-ter the clouds a - way.
For when it's full of my Savior's praise, No e - vil can dwell therein.
And if I faith-ful-ly sing His praise, Some others may love Him too.

CHORUS.

I love to sing a-bout Je - sus, I love to sing a-bout Je - sus,

I love to sing a-bout Je - sus, Be-cause He died for me.

No. 39. Hiding, Safely Hiding.

E. O. E. and A. B

E. O. EXCELL.

1. Neath the shadow of th' Al-might-y, In the presence of my King;
2. When the storms of life are rag-ing, Clos-er to His side I cling;
3. All my life, my love, my serv-ice, All I have to Him I bring;

I am hid - ing, hid - ing, Hiding in the shadow of His wing.
I am hiding, safely hiding, hiding, safely hiding, Hiding in the shadow of His wing.

In the se - cret place a - bid-ing, In con-tent-ment I can sing.
In His love I'm safe - ly shel-tered, Peace and qui-et He doth bring.
He will hide me, safe - ly hide me Till in heav'n this song I sing:

I am hid - ing, hid - ing, Hiding in the shadow of His wing.
I am hiding, safely hiding, hiding, safely hiding, Hiding in the shadow of His wing.

FINE.

REFRAIN.

D. S.

Hid - ing, hid - ing, Hiding in the shadow of His wing.
Hiding, safely hiding, hiding, safely hiding, I'm hiding, hiding.

No. 40. The Blood is All My Plea.

Rev. F. C. BAKER.

E. F. MILLER.

1. I knew that God in His Word had spoken, The pow'r of sin can
2. Must I go on in sin and sorrow, To-day in sun-shine,
3. With anguish wrung, I cried, My Lord, Is there not pow'r in
4. Oh, yes, my love will take you in, The blood will cleanse you
5. And there I stand this ver-y hour, Kept by Al-might-y

all be bro-ken, The heart held cap-tive yet be free,
clouds to-mor-row? First I'm sin-ning, then re-pent-ing,
Je-sus' blood To make in me a per-fect cure,
from all sin, Will wash a-way your guilt-y stains,
keep-ing pow'r, Temp-ta-tions come, the blood's my plea,

CHORUS.

Lord, is this bless-ing not for me? The blood, the blood is
Now I'm stub-born, then re-lent-ing.
To cleanse my heart and keep it pure?
And cleanse'till not one spot re-mains.
The precious blood now cleans-es me.

all my plea, Hallelujah! it cleanseth me; Hallelujah! it cleanseth me.

No. 41. 'Tis For You and Me.

E. E. HEWITT. COPYRIGHT, 1894. BY E. O. EXCELL. E. O. EXCELL.

1. There's a par - don full and sweet, 'Tis for you, 'tis for me;
2. There's a peace be-yond all tho't, 'Tis for you, 'tis for me;
3. There's a love no tongue e'er told, 'Tis for you, 'tis for me;
4. There's a help for ev - 'ry day, 'Tis for you, 'tis for me;
5. There's a robe of snow - y white, 'Tis for you, 'tis for me;

Bless - ed rest at Je - sus' feet, 'Tis for you and me.
There's a joy earth nev-er brought, 'Tis for you and me.
There's a wealth of heav-en's gold, 'Tis for you and me.
Strength and bless - ing by the way, 'Tis for you and me.
There's a home of glo - ry bright, 'Tis for you and me.

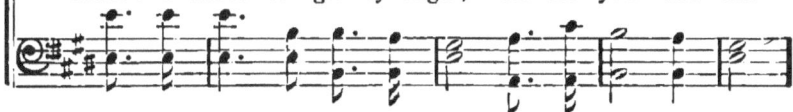

CHORUS.

All for you, if you be - lieve, If sal - va - tion you'll re - ceive,

There's a wel-come, warm and true, All for you, all for me

No. 42.   Oh ! Be Ready.

W. A. O.

W. A. OGDEN.

1. Are you read-y for the Bride-groom's com-ing? Are you read-y
2. Are you read-y for the Bride-groom's com-ing? Has the sum-mons
3. Are you read-y for the Bride-groom's com-ing? Are you go-ing

now the feast to share? Is your lamp all trimm'd and bright, Sending
reach'd a list - 'ning ear? Are you watching all the day, For the
forth to meet Him, say? He is com-ing, brother, see, He is

forth a ra-diant light? Do you still the wed-ding gar-ment wear?
Bride-groom on His way? Are you wait-ing till the Lord draws near?
call-ing now for thee; Oh! be read-y, for He comes this way.

CHORUS.

Oh! be ready, when the Bridegroom comes, Bridegroom comes, Whether it be

ev'ning, Or whether it be morning, Oh! be ready when the Bride-groom comes!

No. 43. No Room in the Inn.

A. L. SKILTON.

E. GRACE UPDEGRAFF.

Slow.

1. No beau-ti-ful cham-ber, No soft cra-dle bed, No place but a
2. No sweet con-se-cra-tion, No seek-ing His part, No hu-mil-i-
3. No one to re-ceive Him, No welcome while here, No balm to re-

man-ger, No-where for His head; No prais-es of glad-ness,
a-tion, No place in the heart; No tho't of the Sav-ior,
lieve Him, No staff but a spear; No seek-ing His treas-ure,

No tho't of their sin, No glo-ry but sad-ness, No room in the inn.
No sor-row for sin, No pray'r for His fa-vor, No room in the inn.
No weep-ing for sin, No do-ing His pleasure, No room in the inn.

CHORUS.

No room, no room for Je-sus, Oh, give Him wel-come free, Lest

rit.

you should hear at heav-en's gate, "There is no room for thee."

No. 44. Go Forward, O Worker.

W. A. O.   WORDS AND MUSIC.   W. A. OGDEN.

1. Go for-ward, O work - er for Je - sus! Thy du - ty be -
2. Go for-ward, O work - er for Je - sus! Lo! yon - der a -
3. Go for-ward, O work - er for Je - sus! The world for the
4. Go for-ward, O work - er for Je - sus! Thy ser - vice He'll

fore thee is   plain, A field for thy   la - bor is   o - pen,
wait-ing there stands, The work which the Mas-ter hath giv'n thee,
Mas-ter to   win; Go tell of His wond'rous sal - va - tion,
glad-ly re - ward; A crown of re - joic - ing He giv - eth

CHORUS.

And Je - sus is   call - ing   a - gain.
Go la - bor as   Je - sus com - mands.   A - rise! the Mas-ter's
To souls that are   dy - ing in   sin.
To those who be - lieve   on His   word.

call o - bey, And to His vineyard haste a - way; Go la - bor

while 'tis called to - day, For soon the night com-eth a - gain.

No. 45. Jesus is Waiting to Save.

E. O. E.

E. O. EXCELL.

1. Why do you linger in darkness so long? Jesus is waiting to save;
2. Leave the broad road and the narrow way choose, Jesus is waiting to save;
3. Time will not linger; how soon we must go! Jesus is waiting to save;
4. Je - sus is calling, oh, come un-to me! Jesus is waiting to save;
5. While we are praying, oh, stay not a - way, Jesus is waiting to save;

save you now;

Have you not friends in the heavenly throng? Jesus is waiting to save.
An-gels are long-ing to tell the glad news, Jesus is waiting to save.
Why turn away, and to Je-sus say, No? Jesus is waiting to save.
Par-don is purchased, sal - va - tion is free, Jesus is waiting to save.
Come to Him now, not a mo-ment de-lay, Jesus is waiting to save.

save you now.

CHORUS.

Come to Him now, come to Him now, Je - sus is wait-ing to save;

save you now:

Come to Him now, come to Him now, Je - sus is wait-ing to save.

save you now.

No. 46. Remember, Keep Holy.

W. A. O.

W. A. OGDEN.

1. If you meet a comrade on the Sabbath day, Who would seek to lead you
2. If a-long the highway, or the busy street, Lit-tle Sabbath breakers
3. In the world around you, in the sky above, There are hearts to cheer you,

in-to paths a-stray, Be a lit-tle he-ro, and your courage show,
you should chance to meet, Be a lit-tle Christian, do not with them go,
there are souls to love, Fol-low in the path-way of your Lord be-low.

CHORUS.

Tell him ver-y plain-ly No! No! no! no! I can-not go,
Let your ac-tion tell them No!
Nev-er from the right way go.

'Tis the Lord's command and I'll o-bey, In his word I read it,

'Twas the Lord who said it, "Remember, keep holy, the Sabbath day."

No. 47. Gather Them In.

COPYRIGHT, 1896, BY E. O. EXCELL.
WORDS AND MUSIC.

H. A. L.   HENRY A. LEWIS.

1. Gath-er the chil-dren in days of youth, Gath-er them in,
2. Gath-er the chil-dren from out the streets, Gath-er them in,
3. Gath-er the chil-dren from scenes of strife, Gath-er them in,

Gath - er them in; Teach them the right way, the way of Truth,
Gath - er them in; In from the hov - els and dark re - treats,
Gath - er them in; Gath - er them in - to the Way of Life,

CHORUS.

Gath-er the chil - dren in. Gath - - er them in, ...
Gath-er the chil - dren in.
Gath-er the chil - dren in. Gath-er them in, gath-er them in,

Gath - - er them in, ... Gath - er them
Gath - er them in, gath - er them in,

in for the gar - ner a - bove, Gath-er the chil-dren in.

No. 48.   Unto Us a Child is Born.

HARRY SANDERS.

1. Un-to us a Child is born, Un-to us a Son is giv'n;
2. Oh, that by a wor-thy song We might ech-o back the strain,
3. Great Redeemer, thou hast died; Thou hast wrought the work sublime:
4. *Won-der-ful* thy name we call, *Coun-sel-lor,* to thee we bow:

Child-the mark of hu-man scorn; Son-the heir of earth and Heav'n;
Erst that greeted, loud and long, Beth-le-hem's as-ton-ished plain!
And the words have ech-oed wide To the far-thest bounds of time—
Might-y God, the Lord of all, *Fa-ther Ev-er-last-ing*—thou,

Son of God, a hu-man child; *God with us,* his wondrous name;
Might the man-ger cra-dled King With the shepherd watch be-hold,
"It is finished!"—fin-ished long Is thy great Re-demp-tion plan;
Prince of Peace: thy stead-fast throne, Strong in judg-ment stands for aye:

Ho-ly, harmless, un-de-filed; Yet or-dain'd to death and shame.
And with star-led sa-ges bring Frankincense, and myrrh, and gold!
And we bless thee in our song, Lord of an-gels, Son of man!
Ev-'ry land thy might shall own, All thy scep-tre shall o-bey.

No. 49. Follow Thee.

Rev. JOHNSON OATMAN, Jr.   COPYRIGHT, 1895, BY E. O. EXCELL.   E. O. EXCELL.

1. Sav-ior, I will fol-low Thee, Fol-low till the day is done,
2. Sav-ior, I will fol-low Thee, Tho' it lead me to the cross,
3. Sav-ior, I will fol-low Thee, Tho' it lead thro' toil and tears,
4. Sav-ior, I will fol-low Thee, Fol-low till the march is o'er,

Fol-low till the race is run, Fol-low till the crown is won,
Tho' it lead to earth-ly loss, Count-ing all things else but dross,
Tho' it lead thro' wea-ry years, E'en till heav-en's dawn ap-pears,
Fol-low till I reach that shore, Where I'll en-ter heaven's door,

CHORUS.

Sav-ior, I will ev-er fol-low, fol-low Thee. Fol-low Thee, I will

fol-low Thee, All the way I will fol-low Thee, Thou my
ev-er fol-low Thee, All the way I'll fol-low, I will fol-low Thee,

hope, my on-ly plea, Sav-ior, I will ev-er fol-low, fol-low Thee.

No. 50. Heaven's Gates Will Open Wide.

J. Calvin Bushey.

1. A doub - ly pi - ous way con -sists When we our trib - ute
2. That when a hand we kind - ly touch, With pity - ing help or
3. That when our voice in kind be - half Of an - y grief is

bring, In rec - ol - lect - ing God ex - ists In
care; 'Tis known in heav - en just as much, As
heard,Heav'n's won - drous gold - foiled pho - no - graph, Is

Chorus.

ev - 'ry liv - ing thing. Kind words........ can
if we did it there.
tak - ing ev - 'ry word. Kind words and deeds can

nev - er die; To souls....... sweet peace im - part;Heav'n's
wea - ry souls

gates will sure - ly o - pen wide, To him who cheers a heart.

No. 51. Will You Be Washed in the Blood?

E. O. E.

E. O. EXCELL.

1. List, the Spir - it calls to thee, Will you be washed in the blood?
2. Sin - ner, now this blessing claim, Will you be washed in the blood?
3. He can wash you white as snow, Will you be washed in the blood?
4. Christ did drink that cup for all, Will you be washed in the blood?

Je - sus died to make you free, Will you be washed in the blood?
Thro' the dear Re-deem-er's name, Will you be washed in the blood?
And the wit - ness you may know, Will you be washed in the blood?
Don't re - ject the Spir - it's call, Will you be washed in the blood?

Par - don free - ly giv - en, Cleansing you for heav - en.
Claim him as your Sav - ior, He can save for - ev - er.
You can know the hour Of his dy - ing pow - er.
Grace is all a - bound - ing, Joy thro' heav'n re - sound - ing.

CHORUS.

Will you be washed, Washed in the blood of the Lamb
Will you be washed in the blood of the Lamb,

Will you be washed, . . . Washed in the blood of the Lamb.
Will you be washed in the blood of the Lamb,

No. 52. Blessed Assurance.

F. J. CROSBY. COPYRIGHT, 1873, BY JOS. F. KNAPP. BY PER. Mrs. JOS. F. KNAPP.

1. Bless-ed as - sur-ance, Je - sus is mine! Oh, what a fore - taste of
2. Per-fect sub-mis-sion, per-fect de - light, Vis-ions of rap - ture now
3. Per-fect sub-mis-sion, all is at rest, I in my Sav - ior am

glo - ry di - vine! Heir of sal - va-tion, purchase of God, Born of His
burst on my sight, An-gels descending, bring from a - bove Ech-oes of
hap-py and blest, Watching and waiting, look-ing a-bove, Fill'd with His

CHORUS.

Spir - it, washed in His blood. This is my sto - ry, this is my
mer - cy, whis-pers of love.
good-ness, lost in His love.

song, Prais-ing my Sav - ior all the day long; This is my

sto - ry, this is my song, Prais-ing my Sav-ior all the day long.

No. 53.   Mighty to Save.

E. O. E.   E. O. EXCELL.

1. Have you found a   hid-ing place, Je - sus is might-y to save;
2. Tho' your way be dark as night, Je - sus is might-y to save;
3. Sin - ner, at the mer-cy seat, Je - sus is might-y to save;
4.   O the joy, the peace di-vine, Je - sus is might-y to save;

Where the soul can   taste His grace ? Je-sus is might-y to save.
He can make your pathway bright Je-sus is might-y to save.
Seek His par-don, 'tis so sweet, Je-sus is might-y to save.
O the rap-ture, He is mine, Je-sus is might-y to save.

Mighty   to save you from all sin, Mighty to keep you pure within,
Mighty   to lead you in the way, Mighty to bless you day by day,
Mighty   to bid thy sor-row cease, Mighty to give thy soul re-lease,
Mighty   to free-ly jus - ti - fy, Mighty to sweet-ly sanc-ti-fy,

Mighty   to help you, call on Him, Je-sus is mighty to save.
Mighty   to be thy Rock and Stay, Je-sus is mighty to save.
Mighty   to make thy joys in-crease, Je-sus is mighty to save.
Mighty   to ful - ly sat - is - fy, Je-sus is mighty to save.

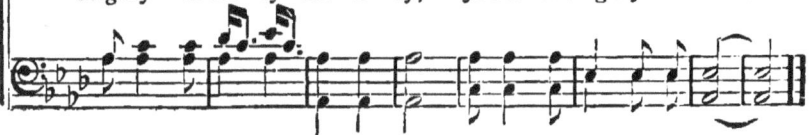

No. 54. Loyalty to Christ.

Dr. E. T. CASSEL. COPYRIGHT, 1894, 1896, BY E. O. EXCELL. WORDS AND MUSIC. FLORA H. CASSEL.

1. Up - on the western plain There comes the signal strain, 'Tis loy-al-ty,
2. O hear ye brave the sound That moves the earth around 'Tis loy-al-ty,
3. Come, join our loyal throng We'll rout the giant wrong, 'Tis loy-al-ty,
4. The strength of youth we lay At Je-sus' feet to - day, 'Tis loy-al-ty,

loy - al - ty, loy - al - ty to Christ; Its mu - sic rolls a - long, The
loy - al - ty, loy - al - ty to Christ; A - rise to dare and do, Ring
loy - al - ty, loy - al - ty to Christ; Where Satan's banners float, We'll
loy - al - ty, loy - al - ty to Christ; His gos - pel we'll proclaim, Thro'

FINE.

hills take up the song, Of loy - al - ty, loy-al-ty, Yes, loy-al-ty to Christ.
out the watch-word true, Of loy - al - ty, loy-al-ty, Yes, loy-al-ty to Christ.
send the bu-gle note, Of loy - al - ty, loy-al-ty, Yes, loy-al-ty to Christ.
out the world's domain, Of loy - al - ty, loy-al-ty, Yes, loy-al-ty to Christ.

CHORUS. D. S.—*Thro' loy - al - ty, loy-al-ty, Yes, loy-al-ty to Christ.*

"On to vic - to-ry! On to vic-to-ry!" Cries our great Commander;

D. S.

"On!" . . . . . We'll move at His command, We'll soon possess the land,

No. 55. Rejoice, Rejoice, the Lost is Found.

F. L. B. COPYRIGHT, 1889, BY E. O. EXCELL. FRANK L. BRISTOW.

1. Joyfully march a-long, and shout the song To the earth's re-mot-est
2. Wanderer far a - way from love to - day, In the sea of sin so
3. Joyfully an - gels bring the sig - net ring, Of a Father's pard'ning
4. Heavenly home! Sweet home! How sweet to roam thro' thy realm of beauty

bound, "Salvation's come, The wand'rer's home, The lost one now is found,"
low, A call from home now bids you "come," Arise and say "I'll go."
grace, And royal fare, they now prepare, Be-fore His smiling face,
rare, With angel throng, join in a song Of joy beyond compare.

Re - joice! Rejoice! with heart and voice; Repeat the welcome sound!
Your va - cant chair is wait-ing there, And raiment white as snow!
A - way with fears! a - way with tears! Receive His fond em-brace!
"Redeemer!" "King!" for-ev-er sing The loved ones gathered there!

CHORUS.

With songs of joy, Your tongues employ, And repeat the welcome sound,

1 2

"Salvation's come! The wand'rer's home, The lost one now is found; now is found!"

No. 56. Onward, Christian Soldiers!

SABINE BARING-GOULD.　　　　　　　　Arr. by SULLIVAN.

1. On-ward Christian sol-diers! march-ing as to war, With the cross of
2. At the sign of tri-umph Satan's host doth flee; On then, Christian
3. Like a might-y ar-my moves the Church of God; Brothers, we are
4. On-ward, then, ye people, Join our hap-py throng, Blend with ours your

Je - sus Go-ing on be-fore; Christ, the roy-al Mas-ter, Leads a-
sol - diers, On to vic - to - ry! Hell's foundations quiv-er At the
treading Where the saints have trod; We are not di - vi - ded, All one
voic - es In the triumph song; Glo - ry, laud and hon-or Un-to

gainst the foe; Forward in - to bat - tle, See His ban-ner go!
shout of praise; Brothers, lift your voic-es, Loud your anthems raise.
bod - y we, One in hope and doc-trine, One in char - i - ty.
Christ, the King, This thro' countless a - ges Men and an - gels sing.

CHORUS.

On-ward, Chris-tian sol - diers! Marching as to war,

With the cross of Je - sus Go-ing on be - fore.

No. 57.　How Firm a Foundation.

GEORGE KEITH.　　　PORTUGUESE HYMN.　　　M. PORTOGALLO.

1. How firm a foun-da-tion, ye　saints of the　Lord,　Is　laid for your
2. "Fear not,　I am with thee, O　be　not dis-mayed, For　I　am thy
3. "When thro' the deep waters I　call thee to　go,　The riv - ers of
4. "The soul that on　Je-sus hath leaned for re - pose,　I will not, I

faith in His ex - cel-lent word! What more can He say, than to
God, I will still　give thee aid;　I'll strengthen thee, help thee, and
sor - row shall not　o - ver-flow;　For　I　will be　with thee thy
will not de - sert　to his foes;　That soul, tho' all hell should en-

you He hath said,　To　you, who for　re - fuge to　Je - sus have
cause thee to　stand, Up - held by my gra-cious, om - nip - o - tent
tri - als to　bless, And　sanc - ti - fy　to　thee thy deep-est dis -
deav - or to　shake, I'll　nev-er, no nev - er, no　nev - er for -

fled? To　you, who for　re - fuge to　Je - sus have fled?
hand, Up - held by my　gra - cious, om - nip - o - tent hand.
tress, And　sanc - ti - fy　to　thee thy deep - est　dis - tress.
sake, I'll　nev - er, no　nev - er, no nev - er　for-sake!"

No. 58. My Father Knows.

S. M. I. HENRY.

E. O. EXCELL.

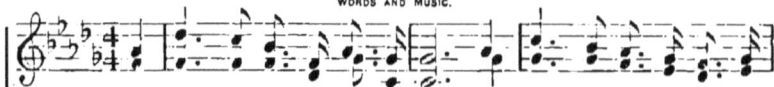

1. I know my heav'nly Father knows The storms that would my way op-
2. I know my heav'nly Father knows The balm I need to soothe my
3. I know my heav'nly Father knows How frail I am to meet my
4. I know my heav'nly Father knows The hour my journey here will

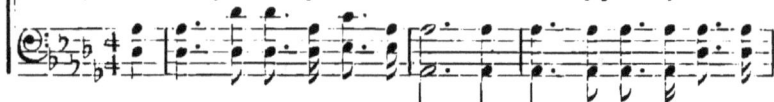

pose. But He can drive the clouds a - way, And turn my
woes; And with His touch of love di - vine, He heals this
foes, But He my cause will e'er de - fend, Up - hold and
close, And may that hour, O faith - ful Guide, Find me safe

dark-ness in - to day, And turn my darkness in - to day.
wounded soul of mine, He heals this wounded soul of mine.
keep me to the end, Up - hold and keep me to the end.
shel-tered by Thy side, Find me safe sheltered by Thy side.

CHORUS.

He knows, He knows The storms that would my way oppose;
My Father knows, I'm sure He knows, That would my way oppose;

My Father Knows. Concluded.

He knows, He knows, And tempers ev'ry wind that blows.
My Father knows, I'm sure He knows, ev'ry wind that blows.

No. 59. While Shepherds Watched.

N. TATE.   CHRISTMAS C. M.   G. F. HANDEL.

1. While shepherds watched their flocks by night, All seated on the ground,
2. "Fear not," said He for might-y dread Had seized their troubled mind,—
3. "To you, in Da-vid's town, this day, Is born of Da - vid's line,
4. The heav'nly babe you there shall find To hu-man view dis - played,

The an - gel of the Lord came down, And glo - ry shone a - round,
"Glad ti-dings of great joy I bring To you and all man - kind,
The Sav-ior, who is Christ, the Lord; And this shall be the sign:
All mean-ly wrapp'd in swath - ing bands And in a man - ger laid.

And glo - ry shone a - round.
To you and all man - kind.
And this shall be the sign:
And in a man - ger laid."

5 Thus spake the seraph; and forthwith
Appeared a shining throng
Of angels, praising God, and thus
Addressed their joyful song:

6 "All glory be to God on high,
And to the earth be peace;
Good-will henceforth from heav'n to men
Begin and never cease!"

No. 60. Improve the Golden Moments.

Rev. F. L. SNYDER.

E. O. EXCELL.

1. O im-prove the gold-en moments, As they quickly come and go.
2. O im-prove the gold-en moments, As they come to you each day,
3. O im-prove the gold-en moments, Be a help in time of need;

For the world is full of sor-row, There are man - y souls in woe;
Scat - ter seeds of truth and kindness All a - long the pil-grim way;
Hast-ing to the weak and fall-en, To their res - cue quickly speed,

Tis no time for i - dle wait - ing, Asking what there is to do;
Thus you cheer some struggling sol - dier, Or you help a soul in need;
For the mo-ments will not tar - ry, Soon will fall the shades of night,

In the vine-yard of the Mas-ter There is work e-nough for you.
Do not then become discouraged, Christ, the Cap - tain, He will lead.
So what thou wouldst do for Je - sus, Do it now with all your might.

CHORUS.

O im-prove the golden mo-ments, 'Tis the Mas - ter calls for thee,

Improve the Golden Moments. Concluded.

Crowd them full of earnest la - bor, Answer, "Here am I, send me."

No. 61. Beautiful Isle.

COPYRIGHT, 1897, BY E. O. EXCELL.
WORDS AND MUSIC.

JESSIE B. POUNDS.

J. S. FEARIS.

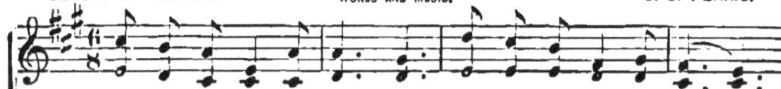

1. Somewhere the sun is shin - ing, Somewhere the song-birds dwell;
2. Somewhere the day is long - er, Somewhere the task is done;
3. Somewhere the load is lift - ed, Close by an o - pen gate;

Hush, then, thy sad re - pin - ing; God lives, and all is well!
Some-where the heart is strong - er, Somewhere, the guer-don won.
Some-where the clouds are rift - ed, Somewhere the an - gels wait!

CHORUS.

Some - where, Some - where, Beau-ti - ful Isle of Some-where!
Some-where beau-ti-ful, beau-ti-ful Isle.

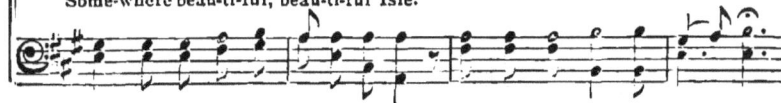

Land of the true where we live a-new,—Beau-ti - ful Isle of Some-where!

No. 62. Go and Find the Wand'rer.

W. A. O.   COPYRIGHT, 1889, BY E. O. EXCELL.   W. A. OGDEN.

1. Go and find the wan-d'rer, Straying from the Father, Go and search the
2. Go and find the wan-d'rer, Go and plead the sto - ry, Of the lov-ing
3. Go and find the wan-d'rer, On the highway roaming, Far a-way from

paths where the weak and err-ing stray, Bring him back to Je - sus,
Sav - ior who died for sin-ful men, Go in faith be-liev - ing
God, and from home, and friends a - way, Bring him back to Je - sus,

To the dear Re-deem-er, Who will take his sins, all his sins a - way.
In the name of Je - sus, Go, and tell the sto-ry of Christ a - gain.
To the lov-ing Sav - ior, Bring him back to God while 'tis called to - day.

CHORUS.

Go and bring him back,   Bring the wand'rer back,   To the fold of God,
Go . . . . and bring the wand - 'rer,   To . . . . the dear Re-

To the fold of God,   Tell him of the Lamb;   Of the bleed-ing Lamb;
deem - er,   Tell . . . . him of the Lamb . . . . of

Go and Find the Wand'rer. Concluded.

rit.

Lamb of God who takes the sins of men a-way.
God who tak - - - eth sin a - way..................

No. 63.   Shall We Meet?

H. L. HASTINGS.   USED BY PERMISSION.   ELIHU S RICE.

1. Shall we meet be-yond the riv-er, Where the surg-es cease to roll?
2. Shall we meet be-yond the riv-er, When our storm-y voyage is o'er?

V.S.   FINE.

Where in all the bright for-ev- er, Sor-row ne'er shall press the soul?
Shall we meet and cast the anchor By the bright ce - les - tial shore?

D.S. *Shall we meet be-yond the riv-er, Where the surg - es cease to roll?*

CHORUS.   D. S.

Shall we meet, shall we meet, Shall we meet be-yond the riv-er?

3 Shall we meet in yonder city,
   Where the towers of crystal shine?
Where the walls are all of jasper,
   Built by workmanship divine.

4 Where the music of the ransomed
   Rolls its harmony around,
And creation swells the chorus
   With its sweet melodious sound.

5 Shall we meet there many a loved one
   That was torn from our embrace?
Shall we listen to their voices,
   And behold them face to face?

6 Shall we meet with Christ our Savior,
   When he comes to claim his own?
Shall we know his blessed favor,
   And sit down upon his throne?

No. 64.   Count Your Blessings.

Rev. J. OATMAN, Jr.
COPYRIGHT, 1897, BY E. O. EXCELL
WORDS AND MUSIC
E. O. EXCELL.

1. When up-on life's bil-lows you are tempest toss'd, When you are dis-
2. Are you ev-er burden'd with a load of care? Does the cross seem
3. When you look at others with their lands and gold, Think that Christ has
4. So a-mid the conflict, whether great or small, Do not be dis-

couraged, thinking all is lost, Count your many blessings, name them
heav-y you are called to bear? Count your many blessings, ev-'ry
promised you His wealth un-told, Count your many blessings, mon-ey
couraged, God is o-ver all, Count your many blessings, an-gels

one by one, And it will surprise you, what the Lord hath done.
doubt will fly, And you will be sing-ing as the days go by.
can-not buy Your re-ward in heav-en, nor your home on high.
will at-tend, Help and comfort give you to your jour-ney's end.

CHORUS.

Count your blessings, Name them one by one, Count your
Count your many bless-ings, Name them one by one, Count your man-y

blessings, See what God hath done, Count your blessings,
bless-ings, See what God hath done, Count your many bless-ings,

Count Your Blessings; Concluded.

Name them one by one, Count your many blessings, See what God hath done.

No. 65. My Happy Home.

ANON.

COPYRIGHT, 1869, BY E. O. EXCELL.

E. O. EXCELL.

1. Je - ru - sa-lem, my hap - py home, O how I long for thee!
2. Thy walls are all of precious stone Most glorious to be - hold;
3. Thy gar-dens and thy pleasant streams, My stud-y long have been—
4. Reach down, reach down thine arms of grace, And cause me to as-cend

When will my sor-rows have an end? Thy joys, when shall I see?
Thy gates are rich - ly set with pearl, Thy streets are pav'd with gold.
Such sparkling gems by hu - man sight Have nev - er yet been seen.
Where con-gre-ga - tions ne'er break up, And prais-es nev - er end.

CHORUS.

I will meet you in the City of the New Je-ru-sa-lem, I am wash'd in the

blood of the Lamb, . . . I am wash'd in the blood of the Lamb.
in the blood of the Lamb,

No. 66. His Glory Fills My Soul.

COPYRIGHT, 1897, BY E. O. EXCELL.

ADAM CRAIG. WORDS AND MUSIC. E. O. EXCELL.

1. O hear me while I tell you what Je - sus did for me,
2. He led me to the foun - tain, and wash'd a - way my sin,
3. He drove out sin and Sa - tan, and filled my heart with love,
4. I nev - er was so hap - py, I'm free from ev - 'ry care,
5. O sin - ner come to Je - sus and to Him bend the knee;

He brought me out of dark - ness, to light and lib - er - ty,
He clothed me in white rai - ment and cleans'd my heart with - in,
He made my an - gry spir - it as gen - tle as a dove,
For Je - sus trav - els with me, my bur - dens all to share,
You can - not buy sal - va - tion, the of - fer's full and free,

He filled my heart with sun-shine, I'm hap - py as can be;
He is my bless - ed Sav - ior; I give my life to Him;
My life o'er-flows with glad-ness, the earth's like heav'n a - bove,
And if I'm faith - ful to Him, a gol - den crown I'll wear,
Up - the cross of Calv - 'ry, He died for you and me;

CHORUS.

His glo - ry fills my soul.
His glo - ry fills my soul.
His glo - ry fills my soul. } His glo-ry, His glo - ry, His glory fills my
His glo - ry fills my soul.
His glo - ry fills my soul

His Glory Fills My Soul. Concluded.

soul, His glo - ry, His glo - ry, His glo - ry fills my soul.

No. 67.   My Body, Soul and Spirit.

COPYRIGHT, 1869, BY JOSEPH F. KNAPP   BY PER.

MARY D. JAMES.   Mrs. JOSEPH F. KNAPP.

1. My bod - y, soul and spir - it,   Je - sus,   I give to   Thee,
2. O, Je - sus, might - y Sav - ior,   I trust in Thy great   name,
3. O, let the fire   descend-ing Just now up - on   my   soul,
4. I'm Thine, O bless - ed Je - sus, Wash'd by Thy cleansing blood;

A con - se - cra - ted of - f'ring Thine ev - er - more   to   be.
I look   for Thy sal - va - tion, Thy prom - ise now   I   claim.
Consume my hum - ble of - f'ring, And cleanse and make me   whole.
Now seal   me   by Thy Spir - it,   A   sac - ri - fice   to   God.

CHORUS.

My all   is   on   the   al - tar,   I'm wait-ing   for   the   fire;

rit.

Wait-ing,   wait-ing,   wait - ing,   I'm wait-ing   for   the   fire.

No. 68.　　I Feel Like Going On.

E. A. H.　　　　COPYRIGHT, 1887, BY E. O. EXCELL.　　　ELISHA A. HOFFMAN.

[In a testimony meeting a Christian in the prime of life spoke of his many trials and discouragements, and seemed utterly down-cast. Following him, an old gray-haired father arose to his feet, and in clear, thrilling tones, cried: "Brethren, I feel like going on, the Lord being my help." His words proved an inspiration to every heart.]

1. I am a Chris-tian pil-grim, And jour-ney to a land,
2. Why should I be dis-cour-aged, Tho' oft the sky ap-pears
3. I meet with ma-ny troub-les, And tri-als on the way;

Where, robed in roy-al gar-ments, The Lord's an-noint-ed stand;
All veiled in clouds and dark-ness, And I have doubts and fears?
But when I look to Je-sus, And in the spir-it pray,

In Je-sus' blood, these saved ones Have wash'd their garments white,
My Lord and my Re-deem-er, While he my lead-er is,
He gives me grace and cour-age And helps my soul a-long;

And soon I hope to join them, In yon-der land of light.
Will guide my steps in safe-ty, What want I more than this?
And so I go re-joic-ing, And sing my pil-grim song.

I Feel Like Going On. Concluded.

CHORUS.

I feel like go-ing on, broth-er, I feel like go - ing on,

I'm on my way to Zi - on, And I feel like go-ing on.

No. 69. All to Christ I Owe.

Mrs. E. M. HALL. USED BY PERMISSION. JOHN T. GRAPE.

1. I hear the Sav-ior say, Thy strength indeed is small; Child of
2. Lord, now in-deed I find Thy pow'r and Thine a - lone, Can
3. For noth-ing good have I Where - by Thy grace to claim—I'll
4. When from my dy-ing bed My ransomed soul shall rise, Then
5. And when be-fore the throne I stand in Him com-plete, I'll

CHORUS.

weakness, watch and pray, Find in me thine all in all. Je - sus paid it
change the leper's spots, And melt the heart of stone.
wash my garments white In the blood of Calvary's Lamb.
"Je-sus paid it all" Shall rend the vaulted skies.
lay my trophies down, All down at Je - sus' feet.

all, All to Him I owe; Sin had left a crimson stain, He washed it white as snow.

No. 70. We Shall Stand Before the King.

E. O. E.

E. O. EXCELL.

1. We shall stand be-fore the King, With the an - gels we shall sing,
2. Ring, ye bells of heav-en, ring, We shall stand before the King,
3. Wake, my soul, thy tribute bring, Thou shalt stand before the King,

By and by, ... by and by, Walk the bright, the golden shore,
By and by, ... by and by. There our sor-rows will be o'er,
By and by, ... by and by! Lay thy tro-phies at His feet,

By and by, by and by.

Prais-ing Him for-ev - er-more, By and by, . . . by and by.
There His name we will a - dore, By and by, . . . by and by.
In His likeness stand complete, By and by, . . . by and by.

By and by, by and by.

CHORUS.

We shall stand, . . before the King, . . . With the angels we shall

We shall stand   before the King,

sing, Glo-ry, glo - ry to our King, Hal-le - lu - - - jah, hal - le -

Hal - le - lu - jah,

We Shall Stand Before the King. Concluded.

lu - jah, We shall stand . . . . . be-fore the King.
Hal - le - lu - jah, We shall stand

No. 71.   Jesus Is Passing By.

E. A. H.   COPYRIGHT, 1894, BY E. O. EXCELL.   Rev. E. A HOFFMAN.

1. This is the sea-son of hope and grace, Je-sus is pass-ing by;
2. This is the hour for the soul's re-lease, Je-sus is pass-ing by;
3. This is the mo-ment to seek the Lord, While He is pass-ing by;
4. Trust in the Lord in this hour of need, While He is pass-ing by;

This, for sal - va-tion the time and place, Je-sus is pass-ing by.
Trust Him and thou shalt go forth in peace, Je-sus is pass-ing by.
This is the time to be-lieve His word, While He is pass-ing by.
And you will find Him a friend in-deed, Je-sus is pass-ing by.

CHORUS.

Je-sus is pass-ing by, Je-sus is pass-ing by;

Bring Him thy heart ere in grief He depart; Je-sus is pass-ing by

No. 72. As We've Sown so Shall We Reap.

F. M. D.

F. M. DAVIS

1. As we've sown so shall we reap, When the harvest time appears,
2. As we've sown so shall we reap, In the tide of com - ing years,
3. As we've sown so shall we reap, When the fields are read-y, white,

Wheth-er it be joy or glad-ness, weal or woe, This the
Reap-ing fruits of sin - ful life, or time well spent, Then this
And the Mas-ter calls for reap-ers here be - low, Let us

thought for us to keep, As through life we on-ward move,
thought in view still keep, While the hours are go - ing by,
then this thought still keep, While the trum - pet call is heard,

We shall gath - er at the har - vest what we sow.
Shall we sow un - ho - ly strife or sweet con - tent?
Shall we la - den well, or emp - ty hand - ed go?

CHORUS.

On, on, ev - er to the har - vest, Sow-ing ei-ther weal or

As We've Sown so Shall We Reap. Concluded.

woe,
weal or woe,
This the thought for us to keep, As thro'

life we onward move, We shall gather at the harvest what we sow,

No. 73. There is a Fountain.

WILLIAM COWPER.   FOUNTAIN. C. M.   Western Melody.

1. { There is a fountain filled with blood, Drawn from Immanuel's veins, }
    { And sinners plunged beneath that flood, (*Omit.*) }   Lose

D.C.—*And sinners plunged beneath that flood,*   (*Omit.*)   *Lose*

FINE.   D. C.

all their guilty stains. Lose all their guilty stains, Lose all their guilty stains.
all their guilty stains.

2 The dying thief rejoiced to see
    That fountain in his day;
    And there may I, tho' vile as he,
    Wash all my sins away.   [blood

3 Dear dying Lamb! Thy precious
    Shall never lose its power,
    Till all the ransomed Church of God
    Are saved to sin no more.

4 E'er since by faith, I saw the stream
    Thy flowing wounds supply,
    Redeeming love has been my theme
    And shall be, till I die.

5 Then in a nobler, sweeter song,
    I'll sing Thy power to save,
    When this poor lisping. stamm'ring
    Lies silent in the grave. [tongue,   .

No. 74. I Will Not Forget Thee.

C. H. G.   CHAS. H. GABRIEL.

1. Sweet is the prom-ise "I will not forget thee." Nothing can mo-
2. Trust-ing the prom-ise "I will not forget thee," On-ward will I
3. When at the gold-en por-tals I am stand-ing, All my trib-u-

lest or turn my soul a-way; E'en tho' the night be
go with songs of joy and love, Tho' earth de-spise me,
la-tions, all my sor-rows past, How sweet to hear the

dark within the val-ley, Just beyond is shin-ing an e-ter-nal day.
tho' my friends for-sake me, I shall be re-mem-bered in my home above.
blessed proc-la-ma-tion "Enter, faith-ful ser-vant, wel-come home at last."

CHORUS.

I.................. will not for-get thee or leave thee, In my hands I'll
I will not for-get thee; I will nev-er leave thee,

hold thee, in my arms I'll fold thee I.................. will not for
I will not for-get thee;

I Will Not Forget Thee. Concluded.

get thee or leave thee; I am thy Re-deem-er, I will care for thee.

No. 75.   Let Your Light Shine,

ANNA D. BRADLEY.

J. H. ROSECRANS.

1. What are you doing, broth-er— Do-ing for Christ to-day? Say, does your
2. Have you a burden lift - ed, Spoken a word of cheer? Filled one sad
3. Have you a lost soul rescued, Helped him the tempter flee, Helped him to

CHORUS.

light shine brighter As you go on your way?
heart with comfort, Banished an anxious fear?
sing in rapture— "Jesus has set me free"?

Let your light shine more and
shine, brother,

more,   Let your light shine more and more,   Let your
more and more,   shine, brother,   more and more,

light shine bright with a steady light, Let your light shine more and more.

No. 76. Follow all the Way.

W. A. O   COPYRIGHT, 1889, BY E. O. EXCELL.   W. A. OGDEN.

1. Oh, I love to think of Je - sus, As He journey'd to and fro,
2. Oh, I love to think of Je - sus, And His prais-es I would tell,
3. Oh, I love to think of Je - sus, As He walk'd up-on the wave,

O'er the bar - ren hills of Ju - dah, In the a - ges long a - go,
How He gave the liv - ing wa - ter To the wom-an at the well,
How the el - e-ments obeyed Him, When the mighty word He gave,

How He heal'd the wayside beggar, How He made the lep-er whole,
How He filled the emp-ty ves-sels, At the marriage feast that day,
Speak the word now to my spir - it, Lord, thy bless-ed peace be still;

How in love He lit the al - tar, On the sin po - lu - ted soul.
How He spake the word of comfort To the poor who throng'd this way.
I would fol-low where Thou leadest, I would mag-ni - fy Thy will.

CHORUS.

I will fol - low where He lead - eth, I will
I will fol-low where He lead-eth   fol-low-where He leadeth.

Follow all the Way. Concluded.

past - - ure where He feed - eth, I will follow, follow,
Pasture where He feedeth, pasture where He feedeth,

fol-low all the way, I will fol - low Je-sus ev-'ry day.
fol - low, fol - low,

No. 77. God is Love.

CHAS. WESLEY.   J. STEVENSON.

1. { Depth of mer-cy, can there be   Mer-cy still re-served for me? }
   { Can my God His wrath for-bear, Me, the chief of sinners spare? }

2. { I have long withstood His grace; Long provoked Him to His face; }
   { Would not hark-en to His calls; Griev'd Him by a thousand falls. }

3. { Now in-cline me to re-pent; Let me now my sin la-ment; }
   { Now my soul re-volt de-plore, Weep, be-lieve, and sin no more. }

REFRAIN. *Faster.*   *Smoothly.*   *Repeat pp.*

{ God is love, I know, I feel; } Je-sus weeps, He weeps and loves me still.
{ Jesus weeps, and loves me still; }

4 Kindled His relentings are;
  Me He now delights to spare;
  Cries, "How shall I give thee up?"—
  Lets the lifted thunder drop.

5 There for me the Savior stands;
  Shows His wounds and spreads His
  God is love, I know, I feel; [hands;
  Jesus weeps and loves me still.

No. 78. All My Class for Jesus.

JULIA H. JOHNSON.

LUCY J. RIDER.

1. My schol - ars all for Je - sus! This be my earnest pray'r,
2. My girls, lighthearted, tho'tless, On trifling thing in - tent,
3. My boys I want for Je - sus, My wayward, wand'ring boys,
4. Lord, be in ev-'ry les-son, Bless ev - 'ry falt'ring word

For they are souls im-mor - tal, En - trust - ed to my care;
These cost a price-less ransom, On these my care be spent,
So full of life and beauty, So charm'd by earthly joys,
My trembling lips may ut - ter, To bring them to the Lord,

For each, the Master car - eth, I long, I long for each,
That each a will-ing handmaid, Be brought to own her Lord,
For them the Savior suf - fer'd, For them, His life was giv'n,
So fleet - ing are the moments, Of op - por-tu - ni - ty!

Grant, Lord, the heav'nly wisdom, These wayward hearts to reach.
"What - e'er He saith" to "do it," O - be - dient to His word.
Lord, by that ransom, help me, Bring all my boys to heav'n.
Oh, Je - sus, Mas-ter, help me, Bring all my class to Thee.

All, all my class for Je - sus, Oh, which one could I spare;

All My Class for Jesus. Concluded.

All, all my class in heav-en, Let none be missing there!

No. 79. Under the Cross.

WM. McDONALD. COPYRIGHT, 1889, BY E. O. EXCELL. E. O. EXCELL.

1. I am com-ing to the cross; I am poor, and weak, and blind;
2. Long my heart has sighed for thee, Long has evil reigned within;
3. Here I give my all to thee, Friends, and time, and earthly store;

I am counting all but dross, I shall full sal-va-tion find.......
Je - sus sweetly speaks to me, "I will cleanse you from all sin."...
Soul and bod - y thine to be, Whol - ly thine for ev-er - more.....
Hal - le-lu-jah!

CHORUS.

Un - der the cross I lay my sins, Un - der the cross they lie;

Un - der the cross I lay my sins, Un - der the cross I'll die.

No. 80. Jesus the Truth to Light My Way.

F. L. B. *Moderato.* COPYRIGHT, 1889, BY E. O. EXCELL. FRANK L. BRISTOW.

Imitation bells.

1. Sing the tune-ful lay,
   I can nev-er stray
2. In the days of youth,
   By the wa-ters sheen,
3. In the shades of night,
   Then when 'peeps o' day',

Je - sus is the way	To the gold - en strand	
From that pleas - ant way,	While I faith - ful stand,	
Je - sus is my truth!	Foll'wing by his side,	
In - to pas - tures green,	Man - na un - for - seen,	
He will be my light,	He will vig - il keep	
Rounding pil - lows play,	Ev - er will I pray,	

Of the hap-py land. ⎫
Holding to his hand. ⎬
He shall be my guide, ⎫
Dai - ly he'll pro - vide. ⎬
O'er me when a - sleep, ⎫
Truth to Light my Way! ⎬

UNISON.

Hal - le-lu - jah!

DUET. CHORUS. UNISON.

Hal - le - lu - jah! I am in the way, Hal - le - lu - jah!

Jesus the Truth to Light. Concluded.

DUET. CHORUS.

Hal - le - lu - jah! Je - sus saves to - day;............... day!

No. 81. That Sweet Story.

BY PERMISSION.

Mrs. JEMIMA LUKE.   English.

1. I think, when I read that sweet sto - ry of old, When
2. I wish that His hands had been plac'd on my head, That
3. Yet still to His foot-stool in pray'r I may go, And
4. In that beau-ti-ful place He has gone to pre-pare, For

Je - sus was here among men, How He call'd lit -tle chil-dren as
His arms had been thrown a-round me, That I might have seen His kind
ask for a share in His love; And if I thus earn - est - ly
all who are washed and for-giv'n; And man - y dear chil-dren are

lambs to His fold, I should like to have been with Him then.
look when He said, "Let the lit - tle ones come un - to me."
seek Him be - low, I shall see Him and hear Him a - bove:
gath - er - ing there, "For of such is the kingdom of heav'n."

No. 82. We'll be Right, Instead of Wrong.

F. L. B.

FRANK L. BRISTOW.

Moderato.

1. *Boys.* We are Chris-tian Sol - dier Boys,   Do - ing what we can!
2. *Girls.* We are Chris-tian Pil - grim Girls,   Hap-py Pil - grims bright,
3. *Boys.* S - O - L - D - I - E - R,   Sol-dier, spells, you know,
4. *All.* Lit - tle Chris-tian girls and boys,   * No *Hum - bugs* are we;

For   the right we'll make a noise!   Each may be   a *man!*
Like the pret - ty dew-drop pearls   Fall - ing   in   the night,
Girls. P - I - L - G - R - I - M,   Pil - grim, ain't that so?
For   the right we'll make a noise,   Clap-ping hands with glee!

Ev - 'ry heart is   hap - py now,   We'll be *right* in-stead of *wrong,*
We won't wear   a   "Dunc's cap."   We'll be *right* in-stead of *wrong,*
All. We'll re - peat   it   o'er a - gain,   We'll be *right* in-stead of *wrong,*
God will bless us   ev - 'ry one,   If we're *right* in-stead of *wrong,*

* So   we make a   greet - ing *bow*   While we   sing our song!
* Hear our hands go   *clap, clap, clap,*   As   we   sing our song!
* See   us make the   *sign for rain*   As   we   sing our song!
For   the sake of   His dear Son,   Let   us   sing our song!

CHORUS. *In marching time.*

Let us march, march   a-long,   Up the bright and shin-ing way,

We'll be Right, Instead of Wrong; Concluded.

Do - ing what is right to do, Like a lit - tle { soldier / pilgrim } true!

* 1. All bow at the same time at the word "*bow*."
2. All clap hands *three* times in exact time to the music for the words "*clap, clap, clap!*"
3. To make the deaf mute sign for "*rain*," raise both hands to a level with the top of the head, then bring them slowly down to the sides of the body, working the fingers of each hand rapidly.
4. To make sign for "*Humbug*," place the palm of the right hand upon the back of the left, the fingers, interlaced, and then hands directly in front of the body, working the thumbs up and down.

No. 83.   The Road to Heaven:

E. O. EXCELL.

1. { The road to heav'n by Christ was made, With heav'nly truth the rails are laid; / From earth to heav'n the line extends, To life e - ter-nal where it ends. }

CHORUS

{ I'm go-ing home, I'm going home, I'm going home to die no more! / To die no more, to die no more, I'm going home to die no more! }

2 Repentance is the station, then,
Where passengers are taken in;
No fee for them is there to pay,
For Jesus is himself the way.

3 The Bible is the engineer—
It points the way to heaven so clear,
Thro' tunnels dark and dreary here—
It does the way to glory steer,

4 God's love the fire, his truth the steam
Which drives the engine and the train;
All you who would to glory ride,
Must come to Christ—in him abide.

5 Come, then, poor sinner, now is the
At any station on the line;   [time
If you repent and turn from sin,
The train will stop and take you in.

No. 84. How I Love Jesus.

F. H. C. COPYRIGHT, 1894, BY E. O. EXCELL. FLORA H. CASSEL.

1. How I love Je - sus I nev-er can tell, For He first loved me
2. How I love Je - sus I nev-er can tell, For He has freed from
3. How I love Je - sus I nev-er can tell, Let the glad cho - rus

1. How I love I can - not, can-not tell, For He lov'd me
2. How I love I can - not, can-not tell, For He made me
3. How I love I can - not, can-not tell, Let the cho-rus

Oh, so well, Coming from heav'n to suf-fer for me;
Sor-row's spell, Made in my soul the joy-bells to ring;
Prais-es swell, Ring thro' the earth our glad ju - bi-lee;

loved me Oh, so well, Came from heav'n,from heav'n to die for me;
free from sor-row's spell, In my soul made joy - bells, joy - bells ring;
prais - es, prais - es swell, Ring thro' earth,thro' earth our ju - bi - lee;

Wearing the thorns to make me free.
Giv-en me voice His praise to sing,
Je-sus,our Sav - ior, made us free.

Wearing thorns to make me,make me, free. Je-sus, my Sav-ior,
Gave me voice to sing His, sing His praise.Je-sus, so kind, so
Je - sus, bless-ed Sav - ior, made us free. Worthy all hon-or,

CHORUS.

Dying for me, Shall I not love thro' E-ter - ni - ty? How I love
Faithful to me, In Thy dear presence Happy I'll be.
Wisdom and pow'r,Blessing and glo - ry, His ev - 'ry hour.

How I Love Jesus. Concluded.

Je - sus I never can tell, For He first lov'd me Oh, so well.
How I love I can - not, cannot tell, For He lov'd me, lov'd me, Oh, so well.

No. 85.   America.

L. F. SMITH.   NATIONAL HYMN.

1. My coun - try, 'tis of thee, Sweet land of lib - er - ty,
2. My na - tive coun - try, thee, Land of the no - ble free,
3. Let mu - sic swell the breeze, And ring from all the trees
4. Our Fa - thers' God, to Thee, Au - thor of lib - er - ty,

Of thee I sing; Land where my fa - thers died, Land of the
Thy name I love; I love thy rocks and rills, Thy woods and
Sweet free-dom's song; Let mor - tal tongues a-wake, Let all that
To Thee we sing; Long may our land be bright, With freedom's

cres. . . . .

Pil-grims' pride, From ev - 'ry mount-ain's side, Let free-dom ring.
tem-pled hills, My heart with rap-ture thrills, Like that a - bove.
breathe par-take, Let rocks their si-lence break, The sound pro-long.
ho - ly light, Pro - tect us with Thy might, Great God, our King.

No. 86.　　I Cannot Tell Why.

Rev. JOHN McPHAIL.　　　　　　　　　　　　M. L. McPHAIL.

1. I can-not tell why the dear Sav-ior should love me, Or why He should
2. And when I con-sid-er the great con-de-scen-sion, The an-guish en-
3. I look up-on Je-sus sur-round-ed by sin-ners, I look up-on
4. I won-der if an-gels can tell the deep mean-ing, Of love so un-

come from His throne in the sky; I can-not tell why He should
dured in the gar-den at night; His sor-row-ful heart and the
Him as He hangs on the tree; I hear the pe-ti-tion, "Oh,
sel-fish—His dy-ing for me; Or does it not reach far be-

suf-fer to save me,—A sin-ner un-wor-thy and helpless as I.
cup of de-ri-sion, I stand in a-maze-ment to wit-ness the sight.
Fa-ther, for-give them, Forgive them for all they have done unto me."
yond all con-cep-tion, Re-main-ing, for-ev-er, the great mys-ter-y.

CHORUS.

He loves me, I know it, tho' help-less and poor, For noth-ing is

I Cannot Tell Why. Concluded.

plain - er to me, I am sure; But why He should love me to

suf - fer and die, I an-swer, I know not, I can - not tell why.

No. 87. Come, Ye Disconsolate.

THOMAS MOORE.   SAMUEL WEBBE.

1. Come, ye dis-con - so-late, wher-e'er ye lan-guish; Come to the
2. Joy of the des - o-late, light of the stray-ing, Hope of the
3. Here see the bread of life; see wa - ters flow - ing Forth from the

mer - cy-seat, fer - vent - ly kneel; Here bring your wounded hearts,
pen - i - tent, fade - less and pure, Here speaks the Com-fort-er,
throne of God, pure from a - bove; Come to the feast of love;

here tell your an-guish; Earth has no sorrow that heav'n cannot heal.
ten-der - ly say - ing, "Earth has no sorrow that heav'n cannot cure."
come, ev - er knowing Earth has no sorrow but heav'n can remove.

No. 88. Rally! Rally! Rally!

C. H. G.
COPYRIGHT, 1094, BY E. O. EXCELL.
CHAS. H. GABRIEL.

1. Let us ral - ly! ral ly! ral - ly 'round the ban-ner of the cross!
2. Hark! the trum-pet call is sounding o - ver all the land to-day,
3. Hear the bless-ed prom-ise ring-ing o'er the din of earth-ly strife—

Let us raise it high - er, high-er, for it must not suf-fer loss!
Souls are dy - ing, dy - ing, dy - ing—oh, how can we still de - lay?
"Un - to him that o - ver-com-eth I will give a crown of life!"

Are we not the Sav-ior's chos-en, purchased by His love di-vine?
How the faith-ful ones are striv-ing; look! the foe be-gins to yield!
'Tis the voice of Je - sus speaking, voice the sweet-est ev - er heard;

He is call - ing for the faith-ful—ral - ly, ral - ly in - to line!
Glo - ry, glo - ry, hal - le - lu - jah! ral - ly, ral - ly on the field!
Take, oh, take the cross and ral - ly, ral - ly, ral - ly at His word!

CHORUS.

Then a - wake, awake, and rally 'round the cross, a-wake for the bugle is
Then a-wake, a-wake, and ral-ly 'round the cross, a-wake, a-wake, the

Rally! Rally! Rally! Concluded.

sound - ing, Then a - wake, awake and rally 'round the cross,
bu - gle now is sounding, Then a-wake, a-wake, and ral-ly 'round the cross,

Let us ral - ly, ral - ly, ral - ly, Let us ral - ly 'round the cross.

No. 89. Closing Hymn.

COPYRIGHT, 1897, BY E. O. EXCELL.

JAMES EDMESTON.   E. O. EXCELL.

1. Sav-ior, breathe an eve-ning blessing Ere re-pose our spir - its seal;
2. Tho' de-struc-tion walk a-round us, Tho' the ar-rows past us fly,
3. Tho' the night be dark and drear-y, Darkness cannot hide from Thee;
4. Should swift death this night o'ertake us, And our couch become our tomb,

Sin and want we come con-fess-ing; Thou canst save and Thou canst heal.
An-gel guards from Thee surround us, We are safe, if Thou art nigh.
Thou art He who, nev - er wea-ry, Watch-est where Thy peo-ple be.
May the morn in heav'n a-wake us, Clad in light, and deathless bloom.

No. 90.   Come, Holy Spirit.

ISAAC WATTS.   BALERMA, C. M.   Adapted by R. SIMPSON.

1. Come, Ho-ly Spir-it, heav'nly dove, With all Thy quick'ning pow'rs;
2. Look how we grov-el here be-low, Fond of these earth-ly toys:
3. In vain we tune our for-mal songs, In vain we strive to rise:
4. Fa-ther, and shall we ev-er live At this poor dy-ing rate,

Kin-dle a flame of sa-cred love In these cold hearts of ours.
Our souls, how heav-i-ly they go, To reach e-ter-nal joys.
Ho-san-nahs languish on our tongues, And our de-vo-tion dies.
Our love so faint, so cold to Thee, And Thine to us so great?

No. 91.   Just as I Am.

CHARLOTTE ELLIOT.   WOODWORTH. L. M.   WM. BRADBURY.

1. Just as I am! with-out one plea, But that Thy blood was shed for me,
2. Just as I am! and wait-ing not To rid my-self of one dark blot
3. Just as I am! tho' toss'd a-bout, With many a conflict, many a doubt,

And that Thou bidd'st me come to Thee, O Lamb of God! I come! I come!
To Thee, whose blood can cleanse each spot, O Lamb of God! I come! I come!
Fight-ing and fears within, without, O Lamb of God! I come! I come!

4 Just as I am! poor, wretched, blind,
Sight, riches, healing of the mind,
Yea, all I need in Thee to find,
O Lamb of God! I come! I come!

5 Just as I am! Thou wilt receive,
Wilt welcome, pardon, cleanse, relieve
Because Thy promise I believe:
O Lamb of God! I come! I come!

No. 92. Breathe on Me, Breath of God.

EDWIN HATCH. OLMUTZ. S. M. Gregorian Chant.

1. Breathe on me, Breath of God, Fill me with life a - new; That
2. Breathe on me, Breath of God, Un - til my heart is pure, Un -
3. Breathe on me, Breath of God, Till I am whol-ly Thine; Till
4. Breathe on me, Breath of God, So shall I nev - er die; And

I may love what Thou dost love, And do what Thou wouldst do.
til, with Thee, I will one will, To do or to en - dure.
all this earth - ly part of me Glows with Thy fire di - vine.
live with Thee the per - fect life Of Thine e - ter - ni - ty.

No. 93. Jesus, the Very Thought of Thee.

BERNARD OF CLAIRVAUX. HOLY CROSS. C. M. Unknown.

1. Je - sus, the ver - y tho't of Thee With sweetness fills the breast;
2. No voice can sing, no heart can frame, Nor can the mem-'ry find
3. O hope of ev - 'ry con-trite heart, O joy of all the meek,
4. But what to those who find? Ah, this Nor tongue nor pen can show;
5. Je - sus, our on - ly joy be Thou, As Thou our prize wilt be;

But sweet-er far Thy face to see, And in Thy pres-ence rest.
A sweet-er sound than Je - sus' name, The Sav - ior of man-kind.
To those who ask, how kind Thou art! How good to those who seek!
The love of Je - sus, what it is, None but His loved ones know.
In Thee be all our glo - ry now, And through e - ter - ni - ty.

No. 94. I Love Thy Kingdom, Lord.

TIMOTHY DWIGHT.   ST. THOMAS. S. M.   GEO. FREDERICK HANDEL.

1. I love Thy king - dom, Lord, The house of Thine a - bode. The
2. I love Thy Church, O God! Her walls be - fore Thee stand, Dear
3. For her my tears shall fall, For her my pray'rs as-scend, To
4. Be - yond my high - est joy I prize her heav'n-ly ways, Her

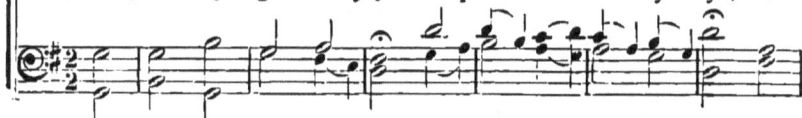

Church our blest Re - deem - er saved With His own pre-cious blood.
as   the ap - ple of Thine eye, And grav - en on Thine hand.
her my cares and toils be giv'n, Till toils and cares shall end.
sweet com-mun-ion, sol - emn vows, Her hymns of love and praise.

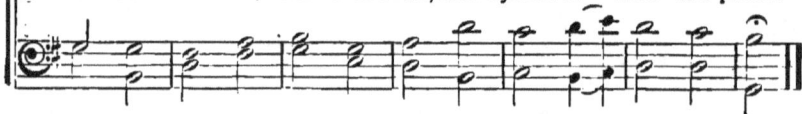

No. 95.   Blest Be the Tie.

JOHN FAWCETT.   DENNIS. S. M   GEO. NAEGELI.

1. Blest be the tie that binds Our hearts in Christian love; The
2. Be - fore our Fa-ther's throne We pour our ar - dent pray'rs; Our
3. We share our mu - tual woes; Our mu-tual bur-dens bear; And
4. When we a - sun - der part, It gives us in - ward pain; But

fel - low - ship of kin - dred minds Is like to that a - bove.
fears, our hopes, our aims are one. Our com-forts and our cares.
of - ten for each oth - er flows, The sym - pa - thiz - ing tear.
we shall still be joined in heart, And hope to meet a - gain.

No. 96. Come, Ye Sinners.

HART.

J. INGALLS.
Fine.

1. { Come, ye sin-ners, poor and need-y, Weak and wounded, sick and sore; }
   { Je-sus read-y stands to save you, Full of pit-y, love and pow'r. }

2. { Now, ye need-y, come and wel-come, God's free bounty glo-ri-fy; }
   { True be-lief and true re-pent-ance, Ev'ry grace that brings you nigh. }

D. C.—*Glo-ry, hon-or, and sal-va-tion, Christ the Lord is come to reign.*

CHORUS.

D. C.

Turn to the Lord, and seek sal-va-tion, Sound the praise of his dear name,

3 Let not conscience make you linger,
Nor of fitness fondly dream;
All the fitness He requireth,
Is to feel your need of Him.

4 Come, ye weary, heavy-laden,
Bruised and mangled by the fall,
If you tarry till you're better,
You will never come at all.

No. 97. Come to Jesus.

1. Come to Je-sus, Come to Je-sus, Come to Je-sus, just now;

Just now come to Je-sus, Come to Je-sus, just now.

2. He will save you.
3. He is able.
4. Only trust Him.

5. Call upon Him.
6. He will hear you.
7. Look to Jesus.

8. He'll forgive you.
9. Don't reject Him.
10. Hallelujah, Amen.

No. 98. Come, Ye That Love the Lord.

ISAAC WATTS.   ARRANGED.

1. Come, ye that love the Lord, And let your joys be known;
2. Let those re - fuse to sing Who nev - er knew our God;
3. There we shall see His face, And nev - er, nev - er sin;
4. Then let our songs a-bound, And ev - 'ry tear be dry;

CHO. *I'm glad sal - va - tion's free, I'm glad sal - va - tion's free;*

Join in a song with sweet accord, While ye surround the throne.
But ser-vants of the heav'n-ly King May speak their joys a-broad.
There, from the riv - ers of His grace, Drink endless pleasures in.
We're marching thro' Immanuel's ground To fair - er worlds on high.

Sal - va - tion's free for you and me; I'm glad sal - va-tion's free.

No. 99. I Do Believe. C. M.

CHAS. WESLEY.   UNKNOWN.

1. Fa - ther, I stretch my hands to Thee, No oth-er help I know;
2. What did Thine on - ly Son en-dure, Be - fore I drew my breath;
3. O Je-sus, could I this be-lieve, I now should feel Thy pow'r;
4. Au - thor of faith, to Thee I lift My wea - ry, long - ing eyes;

CHO. *I do be-lieve, I now be-lieve That Je-sus died for me;*

If Thou with-draw Thy-self from me, Ah! whither shall I go?
What pain, what la - bor to se - cure My soul from end-less death!
And all my wants Thou would'st relieve, In this ac - cept - ed hour.
Oh, let me now re-ceive that gift; My soul with-out it dies.

And thro' His blood, His precious blood I shall from sin be free!

No. 100. How I Love Jesus.

FREDERICK WHITFIELD. Arr. by E. O. E.

*There is a name I love to hear, I love to sing its worth; It
sounds like music in mine ear, The (Omit.) sweetest name on*
earth, Oh, how I love Jesus, Oh, how I love Jesus,
Oh, how I love Jesus, Be- (.Omit.) cause he first lov'd me.

2 It tells me of a Savior's love,
Who died to set me free;
It tells me of His precious blood,
The sinner's perfect plea.

3 It tells me what my Father hath
In store for every day,

And, tho' I tread a darksome path,
Yields sunshine all the way.

4 It tells of One, whose loving heart
Can feel my deepest woe,
Who in each sorrow bears a part,
That none can bear below.

No. 101. Angels Hovering 'Round.

ANON. UNKNOWN.

1. There are an-gels hov'ring 'round, There are an-gels hov'ring 'round,
2. They will carry the tid-ings home; They will carry the tidings home;

There are an - - gels, an - - gels hov - 'ring 'round.
They will car - - ry, car - - ry the tid - ings home.

3 To the new Jerusalem, etc.

4 Poor sinners are coming home, etc.

5 And Jesus bids them come, etc.

6 There's glory all around, etc.

No. 102. From Greenland's Icy Mountains.

HEBER.   MISSIONARY HYMN. 7s. 6s.   MASON.

1. {From Greenland's i - cy mountains, From In-dia's cor - al strand;}
   {Where Af-ric's sun- ny foun - tains, [Omit...................] } Roll

down their golden sand; From many an ancient riv-er, From many a palmy

plain, They call us to de - liv - er, Their land from error's chain.

2 Shall we, whose souls are lighted,
   With wisdom from on high,
Shall we, to men benighted,
   The lamp of life deny?
Salvation! oh, salvation!
   The joyful sound proclaim,
Till earth's remotest nation
   Has learned Messiah's name.

3 Waft, waft, ye winds, His story,
   And you, ye waters, roll,
Till, like a sea of glory,
   It spreads from pole to pole;
Till o'er our ransomed nature,
   The Lamb for sinners slain,
Redeemer, King, Creator,
   In bliss returns to reign.

No. 103.   Jesus, Savior, Pilot Me.   J. E. GOULD.

FINE.

1. Je - sus, Sav - ior, pi - lot me, O - ver life's tempestuous sea;
D. C. *Chart and compass came from Thee; Je - sus, Sav - ior, pi - lot me.*
2. As   a moth - er   stills her child, Thou canst hush the o - cean wild;
D. C. *Wondrous Sovereign of the sea, Je - sus, Sav - ior, pi - lot me.*
3. When at last   I   near the shore, And   the fear-ful break-ers roar,
D. C. *May I hear Thee say to   me, "Fear not, I will pi - lot thee!"*

Jesus, Savior, Pilot Me. Concluded.

D. C.

Unknown waves before me roll, Hid-ing rocks and treacherous shoal;
Boisterous waves o-bey Thy will When Thou sayest to them "Be still!"
'Twixt me and the peaceful rest, Then, while lean-ing on Thy breast,

No. 104. Love Divine, All Love Excelling.

CHARLES WESLEY.   LOVE DIVINE. 8, 7. D.   JOHN ZUNDEL.

1. Love di-vine, all love ex-cell-ing, Joy of heav'n to earth come down!
2. Breathe, O breathe Thy lov - ing spir-it In - to ev - 'ry trou-bled breast;

S.   *FINE.*

Fix in us Thy hum-ble dwelling; All Thy faithful mer - cies crown.
Let us all in Thee in-her-it, Let us find that sec - ond rest.

D.S.—*Vis - it us with Thy sal - va-tion: En -ter ev - 'ry trembling heart.*
D.S.—*End of faith, as its be - ginning, Set our hearts at lib - er - ty.*

D. S.

Je-sus, Thou art all com-passion, Pure un bounded love Thou art;
Take a-way our bent to sin-ning; Al - pha and O - me-ga be;

3 Come, almighty to deliver,
  Let us all Thy life receive;
Suddenly return, and never,
  Never more Thy temples leave:
Thee we would be always blessing,
  Serve Thee as Thy hosts above,
Pray, and praise Thee without ceasing,
  Glory in Thy perfect love.

4 Finish then Thy new creation;
  Pure and spotless let us be;
Let us see Thy great salvation,
  Perfectly restored in Thee:
Changed from glory into glory,
  Till in heaven we take our place,
Till we cast our crowns before Thee,
  Lost in wonder, love, and praise.

No. 105. Come, Thou Fount.

GEO. ROBINSON.

Unknown.

FINE.

1. { Come, Thou Fount of ev-'ry blessing, Tune my heart to sing Thy grace }
   { Streams of mer-cy, nev-er ceas-ing, Call for songs of loud-est praise; }

D. C.—*Praise the mount—I'm fixed upon it! Mount of Thy redeeming love.*

D. C.

Teach me some me-lo-dious sonnet, Sung by flam-ing tongues a-bove.

2 Here I'll raise my Ebenezer,
  Hither by Thy help I'm come;
  And I hope, by Thy good pleasure,
  Safely to arrive at home.
  Jesus sought me when a stranger,
  Wandering from the fold of God,
  He to rescue me from danger,
  Interposed His precious blood.

3 Oh, to grace, how great a debtor,
  Daily I'm constrained to be!
  Let Thy goodness, like a fetter,
  Bind my wandering heart to Thee;
  Prone to wander, Lord, I feel it—
  Prone to leave the God I love—
  Here's my heart, oh, take and seal it,
  Seal it for Thy courts above.

No. 106. God Will Answer Prayer.

W. M. BAILEY.

COPYRIGHT, 1897, BY E. O. EXCELL.
WORDS AND MUSIC.

E. O. EXCELL.

1. Does your way seem dark and drear-y, God will an - swer prayer;
2. Plead your cause, the Lord will heed you, When you bow in prayer:
3. All your sins will be for-giv-en, If you plead in prayer;

Are you heav-y la-den, wea-ry? God will an - swer prayer.
Bread of Life the Lord will feed you, If you ask in prayer.
You may reach a home in heav-en By the way of prayer.

God Will Answer Prayer. Concluded.

Precious promise, oh, how thrilling! Precious promise, each void filling!
Pray to Him your guilt confessing. Pray to Him your love professing,
Sweetest knowledge of cre-a-tion, Trust which leads to con-se-cra-tion,

Precious promise, hope in-still-ing! God will an - swer prayer.
Pray to Him for ev - 'ry bless-ing, God will an - swer prayer.
Pure de-vo - tion and sal-va - tion, God will an - swer prayer.

No. 107.   There's a Widness.

FREDERICK W. FABER.   WELLESLEY, 8s. 7s.   LIZZIE S. TOURJEE.

1. There's a wide-ness in God's mer-cy, Like the wide-ness of the sea,
2. There is wel-come for the sin-ner, And more grac-es for the good.
3. For the love of God is broad-er Than the measure of man's mind;
4. If our love were but more simple, We should take Him at His word;

There's a kind-ness in His justice, Which is more than lib - er - ty.
There is mer-cy with the Sav-ior; There is heal-ing in His blood.
And the heart of the e - ter-nal, Is most won-der-ful - ly kind.
And our lives would be all sunshine In the sweetness of our Lord.

No. 108.   Abide With Me.

H. F. LYTE.

WM. H MONK.

1. A - bide with me! Fast falls the e - ven-tide, The dark-ness
2. Swift to its close ebbs out life's lit - tle day; Earth's joys grow
3. I need Thy pres-ence ev - 'ry pass-ing hour, What but Thy
4. Hold Thou Thy cross be - fore my clos-ing eyes; Shine thro' the

deep - ens—Lord, with me a - bide! When oth - er help - ers
dim, its glo - ries pass a - way; Change and de - cay in
grace can foil the tempter's pow'r? Who like Thy - self, my
gloom and point me to the skies; Heav'n's morning breaks and

fail, and comforts flee, Help of the helpless, oh, a - bide with me!
all around I see; O Thou, who changest not, a - bide with me!
guide and stay can be? Thro' cloud and sunshine, oh, a - bide with me!
earth's vain shadows flee! In life, in death, O Lord, a - bide with me!

No. 109.   O Day of Rest and Gladness.

C. WORDSWORTH.

Arr. by LOWELL MASON.

1. { O day of rest and gladness, O day of joy and light: \
    O balm of care and sad-ness, Most beau-ti - ful most bright; |

2. { On thee, at the cre - a - tion The light first had its birth; \
    On thee, for our sal - va - tion, Christ rose from depth of earth; |

3. { To - day on wea - ry na-tions The heav'n-ly man-na falls; \
    To ho - ly con - vo - ca-tions The sil - ver trumpet calls, |

O Day of Rest and Gladness. Concluded.

On thee the high and low - ly, Thro' a - ges joined in tune,
On thee, our Lord vic - to - rious, The Spir - it sent from heav'n;
Where gos - pel light is glow - ing With pure and ra - diant beams

Sing "ho - ly, ho - ly, ho - ly," To the great God Tri - une.
And thus on thee, most glo-rious, A trip - le light was given.
And liv - ing wa - ter flow - ing With soul re - fresh-ing streams.

No. 110.   Sun of My Soul.

JOHN KEPLER.   HENRY MONK.

1. Sun of my soul, Thou Sav-ior dear, It is not night if Thou be near;
2. When the soft dews of kindly sleep My wearied eye-lids gen-tly sleep,
3. Abide with me from morn till eve, For without Thee I can-not live;
4. If some poor wand'ring child of Thine Hath spurned to-day the voice divine,

O may no earth-born cloud a - rise To hide Thee from Thy servant's eyes.
Be my last tho't, how sweet to rest For-ev - er on my Sav-ior's breast.
Abide with me when night is nigh, For without Thee I dare not die.
Now, Lord, the gracious work begin, Let him no more lie down to sin.

5 Watch by the sick, enrich the poor
With blessings from Thy boundless store
Be every mourner's sleep to-night,
Like infant's slumbers, pure and light.

6 Come near and bless us when we wake,
Ere thro' the world our way we take,
Till in the ocean of Thy love,
We lose ourselves in heaven above.

No. III. O Happy Day.

HAPPY DAY. L. M. PHILIP DODDRIDGE.

1. O hap-py day, that fixed my choice On Thee, my Sav - ior and my God!
2. O hap-py bond, that seals my vows To Him who mer-its all my love!
3. 'Tis done, the great transaction's done, I am my Lord's, and He is mine;
4. Now rest, my long di - vid-ed heart, Fixed on this bliss-ful centre, rest;

Well may this glow - ing heart re-joice, And tell its rap-tures all a - broad,
Let cheer-ful an-thems fill His house, While to that sa-cred shrine I move.
He drew me, and I fol-lowed on, Charmed to confess the voice di-vine.
Nor ev - er from my Lord de-part, With Him of ev - 'ry good possessed.

FINE.

Hap-py day, hap-py day, When Je-sus washed my sins a - way.

D. S.—*Hap - py day, hap-py day, When Je-sus washed my sins a - way.*

D. S.

He taught me how to watch and pray, And live re-joic - ing ev-'ry day.

No. 112. Majestic Sweetness.

SAMUEL STENNETT. ORTONVILLE, C. M. THOMAS HASTINGS.

1. Ma-jes - tic sweetness sits enthron'd Up-on the Sav-ior's brow;
2. No mor-tal can with Him compare, Among the sons of men;
3. He saw me plung'd in deep distress, He flew to my re - lief;

Majestic Sweetness. Concluded.

His head with radiant glories crown'd, His lips with grace o'er - flow,
Fair - er is He than all the fair   That fill the heav'nly   train,
For me He bore the shameful cross And car - ried all my   grief,

His lips with grace o'er - flow.
That fill the heav'nly   train.
And car - ried all my   grief.

4 To heaven, the place of His abode,
He brings my weary feet;
Shows me the glories of my God,
And makes my joy complete.

5 Since from His bounty I receive
Such proofs of love divine,
Had I a thousand hearts to give,
Lord, they should all be Thine.

No. 113.   When I Survey.

ISAAC WATTS.   EUCHARIST. L. M.   ISAAC BAKER WOODBURY.

1. When I survey the wondrous cross, On which the Prince of glo-ry died,
2. For-bid it, Lord, that I should boast, Save in   the death of Christ, my God;
3. See, from His head, His hands, His feet, Sorrow and love flow mingled down;
4. Were the whole realm of nature mine, That were a pres-ent far   too small;

My richest gain I count but loss, And pour con-tempt on all my   pride.
All the vain things that charm me most, I sac - ri - fice them to His blood.
Did e'er such love and sorrow meet, Or thorns compose so rich a   crown?
Love so a - maz-ing, so di-vine, De-mands my soul, my life, my   all.

No. 114. I'm Kneeling at the Mercy-Seat.

(Use any C. M. Metre Hymn with either Chorus.)   ARRANGED.

1. Je-sus, Thine all-vic - to-rious love, Je-sus, Thine all-vic - to-rious love,
CHO. 1. I'm kneeling at the mer-cy - seat, I'm kneeling at the mer-cy - seat,
CHO. 2. I can, I will, I do be-lieve, I can, I will, I do be-lieve,

Je - sus, Thine all vic - to-rious love, Shed in our hearts a - broad;
I'm kneel-ing at the mer - cy-seat, Where Je - sus an-swers pray'r.
I can, I will, I do be-lieve That Je - sus saves me now.

No. 115. Jesus, Thine All-victorious.

1 Jesus, Thine all-victorious love
  Shed in my heart abroad;
  Then shall my feet no longer rove,
  Rooted and fixed in God.

2 Oh, that in me the sacred fire
  Might now begin to glow,
  Burn up the dross of base desire
  And make the mountains flow!

3 Oh, that it now from heav'n might fall
  And all my sins consume!
  Come, Holy Ghost, for Thee I call;
  Spirit of burning, come!

4 Refining fire, go thro' my heart,
  Illuminate my soul;
  Scatter Thy life through every part,
  And sanctify the whole.

No. 116. The Cleansing Wave.

Mrs. PHŒBE PALMER.   BY PERMISSION.   Mrs. JOS F. KNAPP.

1. { Oh, now I see the crimson wave, The fountain deep and wide; }
   { Je - sus, my Lord, mighty to save,   (Omit.) }

2. { I rise to walk in heav'n's own light, A-bove the world and sin, }
   { With heart made pure and, garments white, (Omit.) }

3. { A - maz-ing grace! 'tis heav'n below To feel the blood ap - plied; }
   { And Je - sus, on - ly Je - sus know,   (Omit.) }

The Cleansing Wave. Concluded.

CHORUS.

Points to His wound - ed side.
And Christ enthron'd with - in.
My Je - sus cru - ci - fied.

The cleans-ing stream I
Oh, praise the Lord! it

see! I see! I plunge, and oh, it cleanseth me; }
cleanseth me, It cleanseth me, (*Omit.*) } yes, cleanseth me.

No. 117. At the Fountain.

OLD MELODY.

I. { Of Him who did salvation bring, I'm at the fountain drinking,
   { I could forever think and sing, I'm (*Omit.*) on my journey home.

CHORUS.

Glo - ry to God, I'm at the fountain drinking, on my journey home.

2 Ask but His grace and lo! 'tis given,
I'm at the fountain drinking,
Ask and He turns your hell to heav'n,
I'm on my journey home.

3 Tho' sin and sorrow wound my soul,
I'm at the fountain drinking,
Jesus, Thy balm will make me whole,
I'm on my journey home.

4 Where'er I am, where'er I move,
I'm at the fountain drinking,
I meet the object of my love,
I'm on my journey home.

5 Insatiate to this spring I fly,
I'm at the fountain drinking,
I drink and yet am ever dry,
I'm on my journey home.

No. 118.   Joy to the World.

ANTIOCH, C. M.

Rev. ISAAC WATTS.   Arr. by LOWELL MASON.

1. Joy to the world, the Lord is come! Let earth receive her King; Let ev-'ry

heart pre-pare Him room, And heav'n and na-ture sing,   And

And heav'n and   na-ture

heav'n and na - ture sing,   And heav'n, and heav'n and nature sing.

sing,

And heav'n and na - ture sing.

2 Joy to the world, the Savior reigns,
Let men their songs employ;
While fields and floods, rocks, hills and
Repeat the sounding joy. [plains,

3 No more let sin and sorrow grow,
Nor thorns infest the ground;

He comes to make His blessings flow
Far as the curse is found.

4 He rules the world with truth and
And makes the nations prove [grace,
The glories of His righteousness,
And wonders of His love.

No. 119.   Lord, We Come Before Thee.

WILLIAM HAMMOND.   IGNACE PLEYEL.

1. Lord, we come be-fore Thee now! At Thy feet we humbly bow;
2. Lord, on Thee our souls de-pend, In com-pas-sion now de-scend;
3. In Thine own ap-point ed way, Now we seek Thee, here we stay;
4. Send some message from Thy word, That may joy and peace af-ford;

Lord, We Come Before Thee. Concluded.

O do not our suit dis-dain; Shall we seek Thee, Lord, in vain?
Fill our hearts with Thy rich grace, Tune our lips to sing Thy praise.
Lord, we know not how to go, Till a bless-ing Thou be stow.
Let Thy Spir-it now im-part Full sal-va-tion to each heart.

No. 120. Safely through Another Week.

JOHN NEWTON. SABBATH MORN. 7. 6l. Arr. by L. MASON.

1. { Safe-ly thro' au-oth-er week, God has brought us on our way; }
   { Let us now a bless-ing seek, (Omit.)............................}

2. { While we pray for pard'ning grace, Thro' the dear Re-deem-er's name, }
   { Show Thy re-con-cil-ed face, (Omit.).............................}

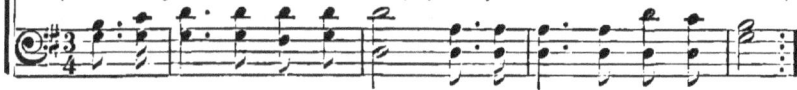

Wait-ing in His courts to-day; Day of all the week the best,
Take a-way our sin and shame; From our world-ly cares set free,

Em-blem of e-ter-nal rest, Em-blem of e-ter-nal rest.
May we rest this day in Thee, May we rest this day in Thee.

3 Here we come Thy name to praise;
  Let us feel Thy presence near.
  May Thy glory meet our eyes,
  While we in Thy house appear;
  Here afford us, Lord, a taste
  Of our everlasting feast.

4 May the gospel's joyful sound
  Conquer sinners, comfort saints;
  Make the fruits of grace abound;
  Bring relief to all complaints;
  Thus may all our Sabbaths prove,
  Till we join the Church above.

No. 121. I am Trusting, Lord, in Thee.

Rev. WM. McDONALD. WM. G. FISCHER.

1. I am com-ing to the cross; I am poor, and weak, and blind;
2. Long my heart has sigh'd for Thee;Long has e - vil dwelt with-in;
3. Here, I give my all to Thee,Friends and time and earthly store,

CHO. *I am trust-ing,Lord, in Thee, Dear Lamb of Cal-va-ry;*

I am count-ing all but dross; I shall full sal-va-tion find.
Je-sus sweet-ly speaks to me,—"I will cleanse you from all sin."
Soul and bod-'y Thine to be— Wholly Thine—for-ev-er-more.

Hum-bly at Thy cross I bow; Save me, Je-sus, save me now.

4. In the promises I trust;
In the cleansing blood confide;
I am prostrate in the dust;
I with Christ am crucified.

5. Jesus comes, He fills my soul!
Perfected in love I am;
I am every whit made whole;
Glory, glory to the Lamb!

No. 122. God's Holy Book.

MARTHA NEWTON.

E. O. EXCELL.

1. What light is this whose constant ray Reveals to trav'lers lost,the way
2. What faithful chart on life's rough sea,What compass true where'er we be,
3. What sword en-a-bles us to fight Against sin's pow'rs and Satan's might,

To mansions of e - ter - nal day? God's holy book, the Bi - ble.
What an-chor for e - ter - nit - y? God's holy book, the Bi - ble.
Gives vic - to - ry for God and right? God's holy book the Bi - ble.

God's Holy Book. Concluded.

CHORUS.

I love the Bi - ble, I love the Bi - ble, A
I love the Bi - ble, I love the Bi - ble,

light to shine up - on my path, I love, I love the Bi - ble.

No. 123.   The Old Time Religion.

UNKNOWN.   ARRANGED.

CHO. 'Tis the old time re - lig-ion, 'Tis the old time re - lig-ion,
1. It was good for our mothers, It was good for our mothers,
2. Makes me love ev - 'ry - bod-y, Makes me love ev - 'ry-bod - y,
3. It has sav - ed our fa-thers, It has sav - ed our fa-thers,

'Tis the old time re - lig - ion, And it's good enough for me.
It was good for our moth-ers, And it's good enough for me.
Makes me love ev - 'ry - bod - y, And it's good enough for me.
It has sav - ed our fa-thers, And it's good enough for me.

4 It was good for the Prophet Daniel,
And it's good enough for me.

5 It was good for the Hebrew Children,
And it's good enough for me.

6 It was tried in the fiery furnace,
And it's good enough for me.

7 It was good for Paul and Silas,
And it's good enough for me.

8 It will do when I am dying,
And it's good enough for me.

9 It will take us all to heaven,
And it's good enough for me.

No. 124. Jesus Bids Us Shine.

E. O. EXCELL.

1. Je - sus bids us shine, With a clear pure light, Like a lit - tle can - dle
2. Je - sus bids us shine, First of all for Him; Well He sees and knows it
3. Je - sus bids us shine, Then for all a - round, Ma-ny kinds of darkness

Burn - ing in the night; In this world of dark - ness,
If our light is dim; He looks down from heav - en,
In this world a - bound, Sin and want and sor - row;

We must shine, You in your small corner, And I in mine.
Sees us shine, You in your small corner, And I in mine.
We must shine, You in your small corner, And I in mine.

No. 125. Where He Leads Me.

E. W. BLANDLY. BY PERMISSION. ARRANGED.

1. I can hear my Sav-ior call-ing, I can hear my Sav - ior call-ing,
2. I'll go with Him thro' the garden, I'll go with Him thro' the garden,
3. I'll go with Him thro' the judgment, I'll go with Him thro' the judgment,
4. He will give me grace and glory, He will give me grace and glo-ry,

CHO. *Where He leads me I will fol-low, Where He leads me I will fol-low,*

Where He Leads Me; Concluded.

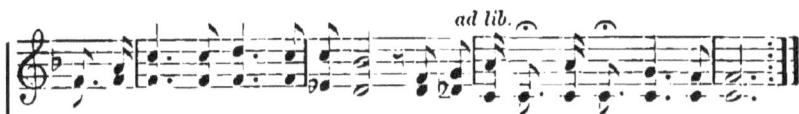

ad lib.

I can hear my Sav-ior calling, "Take thy cross, and follow, follow me."
I'll go with Him thro' the garden, I'll go with Him, with Him all the way.
I'll go with Him thro' the judgment, I'll go with Him, with Him all the way.
He will give me grace and glory, And go with me, with me all the way.

Where He leads me I will fol-low, I'll go with Him, with Him all the way.

No. 126.   There is a Happy Land.

1. There is a hap-py land, Far, far a-way, Where saints in
2. Come to that hap-py land, Come, come a-way, Why will ye
3. Bright in that hap-py land Beams ev-'ry eye; Kept by a

glo-ry stand, Bright, bright as day; Oh, how they sweetly sing, Worthy
doubting stand, Why, still de-lay? Oh, we shall happy be; When from
Fa-ther's hand, Love can-not die; Oh, then, to glo-ry run, Be a

is our Savior, King, Loud let His praises ring, Praise, praise for aye.
sin and sorrow free, Lord, we shall live with thee, Blest, blest for aye.
crown and kingdom won, And bright above the sun We reign for aye.

No. 127.   Revive Us Again.

WM. P. MACKAY.   J. J. HUSBAND.

1, We praise Thee, O God! for the Son of Thy love,
2, We praise Thee, O God! for Thy Spir - it of light,
3, All glo - ry and praise to the Lamb that was slain,
4, All glo - ry and praise to the God of all grace,

For Je - sus who died and is now gone a - bove,
Who has shown us our Sav - ior and scat - tered our night,
Who has borne all our sins and has cleansed ev - 'ry stain,
Who has bought us, and sought us, and guid - ed our ways,

REFRAIN.

Hal - le-lu-jah! Thine the glory; Hal-le-lu-jah! a-men! Re-vive us a-gain,

---

No. 128. God's Love.

Leader:—For God so loved the world, that He gave His only begotten Son, that whosoever believeth in him should not perish, but have everlasting life.

Response:—In this was manifested the love of God toward us, because that God sent His only begotten Son into the world, that we might live thro' Him.

Leader:—Beloved, if God so loved us, we ought also to love one another.

All sing. 1st verse No. 127, We praise, etc.

Leader:—But the Comforter, which is the Holy Ghost, whom the Father will send in my name, he shall teach you all things and bring all things to your remembrance, whatsoever I have said unto you.

Response:—When He, the Spirit of Truth, is come, He will guide you into

God's Love. Concluded.

all truth; for he shall not speak of himself; but whatsoever he shall hear, that shall he speak: and he will show you things to come.

Leader:—He shall glorify me: for he shall receive of mine, and shall show it unto you.

All sing. 2d verse, We praise Thee, etc.

Leader:—And I beheld, and I heard the voice of many angels round about the throne, and the living creatures and the elders; and the number of them was ten-thousand times ten-thousand, and thousands of thousands.

Response:—Saying with a loud voice, Worthy is the Lamb that was slain to receive power, and riches, and wisdom, and strength, and honor, and glory, and blessing.

All Sing. 3d verse, All glory, etc.

No. 129. Holy Spirit, Faithful Guide.

M. M. WELLS.

Fine.

I. { Ho - ly Spir - it, faith-ful Guide, Ev - er near the christian's side, }
{ Gen-tly lead us by the hand, Pil-grims in a des - ert land. }

D. C. *Whispering softly," Wanderer, come, Fol - low me, I'll guide thee home."*

D. C.

Wea - ry souls, for - e'er re-joice, While they hear that sweetest voice

2 Ever present, truest Friend,
Ever, near Thine aid to lend,
Leave us not to doubt and fear,
Groping on in darkness drear.
When the storms are raging sore,
Hearts grow faint and hopes give o'er
Whisper softly,"Wanderer, come,
Follow me, I'll guide thee home."

3 When our days of toil shall cease,
Waiting still for sweet release,
Nothing left but heaven and prayer,
Wondering if our names are there;
Wading deep the dismal flood,
Pleading naught but Jesus' blood;
Whisper softly,"Wanderer, come,
Follow me, I'll guide thee home."

No. 130. Holy Spirit.

Leader:—That which is born of the flesh is flesh; and that which is born of the Spirit is spirit.

Response:—If any man have not the spirit of Christ, he is none of his.

Leader:—As many as are led by the Spirit of God, they are the sons of God.

Response;—The Spirit itself beareth witness with our spirit that we are the children of God.

All Sing: 1st verse, No. 129, Holy Spirit, etc.

Leader;—After that ye believed, ye were sealed with that Holy Spirit of promise, which is the earnest of our inheritance until our redemption of the purchased possessions unto the praise of his glory.

Response.—Grieve not the holy Spirit of God, whereby ye are sealed unto the day of redemption.

Leader;—The Comforter, which is

Holy Spirit. Concluded.

the Holy Ghost, whom the Father will send in my name, he shall teach you all things and bring all things to your remembrance whatsoever I have said unto you.

Response:—The Spirit also helpeth our infirmities, for we know not what we should pray for as we ought, but the Spirit itself maketh intercession for us.

All Sing: 2d verse, Ever present, etc.

Leader:—The fruit of the Spirit is love, joy, peace, long suffering, gentleness, goodness, faith, meekness, temperance; if we live in the Spirit, let us also walk in the Spirit.

Response:—He that soweth to the flesh shall of the flesh reap corruption, but he that soweth to the Spirit, shall of the Spirit reap life everlasting.

All sing: 3d verse, When our days, etc.

No. 131. Blow Ye the Trumpet, Blow.

CHARLES WESLEY. LENOX, H. M. (M. H. 331.)

1. Blow ye the trumpet, blow The glad-ly solemn sound, Let all the nations know, To earth's remotest bound; The year of Ju-bi-lee is come, The year of Ju-bi-lee is come, Re-turn, ye ransomed sin-ners, home.

2 Jesus, our great High Priest,
  Has full atonement made;
  Ye weary spirits, rest;
  Ye mourning souls, be glad;
  ‖:The year of jubilee is come;:‖
  Return, ye ransomed sinners, home.

3 Exalt the Lamb of God,
  The sin atoning Lamb;
  Redemption by his blood
  Through all the world proclaim;
  ‖:The year of jubilee is come;:‖
  Return, ye ransomed sinners, home.

No. 132. Missionary.

Leader.—Go ye, therefore, and teach all nations baptizing them in the name of the Father, and of the Son, and of the Holy Ghost.

Response.—Teaching them to observe whatsoever I have commanded you, and lo, I am with you always even unto the end of the world.

Leader.—All the ends of the world shall remember and . turn unto the Lord, and all the kindreds of the nations shall worship before him.

All Sing. 1st verse, No. 131, Blow ye the trumpet, blow, etc.

Leader.—How then shall they call on him in whom they have not believed? and how shall they believe in him of whom they have not heard? and how shall they hear without a preacher, and how shall they preach except they be sent?

Response.—As it is written, how beautiful upon the mountains are the

Missionary. Concluded.

feet of them that preach the gospel of peace, that bring glad tidings of good things.

Leader.—So shall He sprinkle many nations. He shall see of the travail of His soul and be satisfied for he shall bear their iniquities.

All Sing. 2d verse, Jesus, our great, etc.

Leader.—The wilderness and the solitary place shall be glad for them and the desert shall rejoice and blossom as the rose. It shall blossom abundantly and rejoice even with joy and singing.

Response.—Then shall the lame man leap as an hart and the tongue of the dumb sing, for in the wilderness shall waters break out and streams in the desert.

Leader.—The meek also shall increase their joy in the Lord and the poor among men shall rejoice in the Holy One of Israel.

All Sing. 3d verse, Exalt the Lamb, etc.

No. 133. Guide Me.

W. WILLIAMS.   ZION. 8. 7. 4.   (M. II. 171.)   THOMAS HASTINGS.

1. { Guide me, oh, thou great Jehovah, Pilgrim thro' this barren land; }
   { I am weak but thou art mighty, Hold me with thy pow'rful hand; } Bread of

heaven, Feed me till I want no more; Bread of heaven, Feed me till I want no more.

2 Open now the crystal fountain,
  Whence the healing waters flow;
Let the fiery, cloudy pillar
  Lead me all my journey through:
  ||: Strong Deliverer,
Be thou still my strength and shield.:||

3 When I tread the verge of Jordan,
  Bid my anxious fears subside;
Bear me thro' the swelling current;
  Land me safe on Canaan's side;
  ||: Songs of praises
I will ever give to thee.:||

No. 134. Guide Me.

Leader.—The meek will he guide in judgment; and the meek will he teach his way.

Response.—Thou shalt guide me with thy counsel, and afterward receive me to glory.

Leader.—If I take the wings of the morning, and dwell in the uttermost parts of the sea, even there shall thy hand lead me, and thy right hand shall hold.

All Sing. 1st verse, No. 133, Guide me,

Leader.—I am the living bread which came down from heaven; if any man eat of this bread, he shall live forever.

Response.—When he, the spirit of truth is come, he will guide you into all truth; for he shall not speak of him-

Guide Me. Concluded.

self; but whatsoever he shall hear, that shall he speak; and he will show you things to come.

All Sing: 2d verse, Open now the, etc.

Leader.—Whosoever drinketh of the water that I shall give him shall never thirst; but the water that I shall give him shall be in him a well of water springing up into everlasting life.

Response.—And all the people saw the *cloudy pillar* stand at the tabernacle door; and all the people rose up and *worshiped*; every man in his tent door.

All.—My goodness and my *fortress*; my *high tower*. and my *deliverer*; my *shield*, and he in whom I *trust*.

All Sing: 3d verse, When I tread the, etc.

No. 135. My Faith Looks Up.

RAY PALMER. OLIVET. (M. II. 762.) LOWELL MASON.

1. My faith looks up to Thee, Thou Lamb of Cal-va-ry, Sav - ior di-vine!

{ Now hear me while I pray, } { Take all my guilt a-way, } Oh, let me from this day Be whol-ly Thine.

2 May Thy rich grace impart
Strength to my fainting heart,
   My zeal inspire;
As Thou hast died for me,
Oh, may my love to Thee,
Pure, warm, and changeless be,
   A living fire.

3 While life's dark maze I tread,
And griefs around me spread,
   Be Thou my Guide:

Bid darkness turn to day,
Wipe sorrow's tears away,
Nor let me ever stray
   From Thee aside.

4 When ends life's transient dream,
When death's cold sullen stream,
   Shall o'er me roll;
Blest Savior, then, in love,
Fear and distrust remove;
Oh, bear me safe above,
   A ransomed soul!

No. 136. Faith.

All Sing: 1st verse No. 135, My faith, etc.

Leader:—As many as received him, to them gave he power to become the sons of God, even to them that believe on his name.

Response:—He that believeth on him is not condemned; but he that believeth not, is condemned already, because he hath not believed in the name of the only begotten Son of God.

Leader:—He that believeth on the Son hath everlasting life; and he that believeth not the Son, shall not see life; but the wrath of God abideth on him.

Response:—If ye believe not that I am he, ye shall die in your sins.

All Sing: 2d verse, May Thy rich, etc.

Leader:—And whosoever liveth, and

Faith. Concluded.

believeth in me, shall never die.

Response:—Gracious is the Lord, and righteous; yea, our God is merciful.

Leader:—Even when we were dead in sins, hath he quickened us together with Christ; (by grace ye are saved.)

Response:—That in the ages to come he might show the exceeding riches of his grace in his kindness towards us, through Christ Jesus.

All Sing: 3d verse, While life's dark, etc.

Leader:—Being justified freely by his grace, through the redemption that is in Christ Jesus.

Response.—And if by grace, then it is no more of works; otherwise grace is no more grace.

All Sing: 4th verse, When ends life's etc.

No. 137. My Jesus, I Love Thee.

LONDON HYMN BOOK.   BY PERMISSION.   A. J. GORDON.

1. My Je - sus, I love Thee, I know Thou art mine, For Thee all the
fol - lies Of sin I re - sign; My gra - cious Re - deem-er, My
Sav - ior art Thou, If ev - er I loved Thee, My Je - sus, 'tis now.

2 I love Thee, because Thou
  Hast first loved me,
And purchased my pardon
  On Calvary's tree;
I love Thee for wearing
  The thorns on Thy brow;
If ever I loved Thee,
  My Jesus, 'tis now.

3 I will love Thee in life,
  I will love Thee in death,
And praise Thee as long as
  Thou lendest me breath;

And say when the death-dew
  Lies cold on my brow,
If ever I loved Thee,
  My Jesus, 'tis now.

4 In mansions of glory
  And endless delight,
I'll ever adore Thee
  In heaven so bright;
I'll sing with the glittering
  Crown on my brow,
If ever I loved Thee,
  My Jesus, 'tis now.

No, 138. Love.

Leader.—For all have sinned, and come short of the glory of God.

Response.—But God commendeth his love toward us, in that while we were yet sinners, Christ died for us.

Leader.—And he is the propitiation for our sins; and not for ours only, but also for the sins of the whole world.

Response.—Behold, what manner of love the Father hath bestowed upon us, that we should be called the sons of God.

All Sing 1st verse, No. 137, My Jesus, I love thee, etc.

Love. Concluded.

Leader.—For God so loved the world, that he gave his only begotten Son, that whosoever believeth in him should not perish, but have everlasting life.

Response.—Greater love hath no man than this, that a man lay down his life for his friends.

Leader.—We love him because he first loved us.

All Sing. 2d verse, I love thee because.

Leader.—Hereby perceive we the love of God, because he laid down his life for us: and we ought to lay down our lives for the brethren.

All Sing. 3d verse, I will love thee in, etc.

CHARLES WESLEY.   ITALIAN HYMN, 6s, 4s. (M. H. 6.)   FELICE GIARDINI.

1. Come, thou Al-might-y King, Help us thy name to sing, Help us to praise!

{ Fa-ther all glo - ri-ous, }
{ O'er all vic - to - ri-ous, } Come, and reign o - ver us, Ancient of days.

2 Come, holy Comforter.
Thy sacred witness bear,
In this glad hour.
Thou, who almighty art,
Now rule in every heart,
And ne'er from us depart,
Spirit of power.

3 To thee, great One in Three,
The highest praises be;
Hence, evermore;
Thy sovereign majesty
May we in glory see,
And to eternity
Love and adore.

No. 140.   Praise.

Leader.—I am Alpha and Omega, the beginning and the ending, saith the Lord, which is, and which was, and which is to come, the Almighty.

Response.—O come, let us sing unto the Lord; let us make a joyful noise to the rock of our salvation.

Leader.—O sing unto the Lord a new song; sing unto the Lord all the earth.

All Sing. 1st verse. No. 139, Come, thou Almighty King, etc.

Leader.—Know ye not that ye are the temple of God, and that the spirit of God dwelleth in you.

Response.—Cast me not away from thy presence; and take not thy holy spirit from me.

Leader.—Restore unto me the joy of thy salvation and uphold me with thy free spirit.

Praise. Concluded.

Response.—Then will I teach transgressors thy way; and sinners shall be converted unto thee.

All Sing. 2d verse, Come, holy Comforter,

Leader.—Fear ye not, neither be afraid; have not I told thee from that time, and have declared it? ye are even my witnesses. Is there a God beside me? Yea, there is no God; I know not any.

Response.—For thou art great and doest wondrous things: Thou art God alone.

Leader.—He that overcometh shall inherit all things: and I will be his God, and he shall be my son.

All Sing. 3d verse, To thee, great One in,

No. 141. Rock of Ages.

A. M. TOPLADY.   TOPLADY. 7s.   THOS. HASTINGS.

1. Rock of A - ges, cleft for me, Let me hide my-self in Thee:
D. C. Be of sin the dou-ble cure, Save from wrath and make me pure.

Let the wa - ter and the blood, From thy wounded side which flow'd.

2 Could my tears forever flow,
Could my zeal no languor know,
These for sin could not atone,
Thou must save, and Thou alone:
In my hand no price I bring,
Simply to Thy cross I cling.

3 While I draw this fleeting breath,
When my eyes shall close in death,
When I rise to worlds unknown,
And behold Thee on Thy throne,
Rock of Ages, cleft for me,
Let me hide myself in Thee.

No. 142. Rock of Ages.

Leader:—Behold the Lamb of God who taketh away the sins of the world.

Response:—He was wounded for our transgressions. He was bruised for our iniquity. The chastisement of our peace was upon him, and with his stripes we are healed.

Leader:—Thou shalt call his name Jesus, for he shall save his people from their sins.

All Sing: 1st verse, No.141, Rock of Ages,

Leader:—The blood of Jesus Christ, his Son, cleanseth us from all sin.

Response:—Neither is there salvation in any other, for there is none other name given under heaven among men whereby we must be saved.

Leader:—Without shedding of blood is no remission.

Rock of Ages. Concluded.

Response:—The eternal God is thy refuge and underneath are the everlasting arms.

All sing; 2d verse, Could my tears, etc.

Leader:—The gift of God is eternal life, through Jesus Christ, our Lord.

Response:—By grace are ye saved through faith, and that not of yourselves; it is the gift of God.

Leader:—How shall we escape if we neglect so great salvation.

All.—When thou passest through the waters I will be with thee and through the rivers, they shall not overflow thee; when thou walkest through the fire thou shalt not be burned, neither shall the flame kindle upon thee.

All Sing: 3d verse, While I draw, etc.

No. 143. Jesus, Lover of My Soul.

CHARLES WESLEY. MARTYN. 7 D. (M. H. 656.) S. B. MARSH.

Fine.

> 1. { Je - sus, lov - er of my soul, Let me to Thy bo - som fly, }
> { While the nearer wa-ters roll, While the tempest still is high; }
>
> D. C. *Safe in - to the ha - ven guide, Oh, re-ceive my soul at last.*

D. C.

Hide me, O my Sav - ior, hide, Till the storm of life is past;

2 Other refuge have I none,
  Hangs my helpless soul on Thee;
  Leave, oh, leave me not alone,
  Still support and comfort me.
  All my trust on Thee is stayed,
  All my help from Thee I bring;
  Cover my defenseless head
  With the shadow of Thy wing.

3 Thou, O Christ, art all I want,
  More than all in Thee I find;
  Raise the fallen, cheer the faint,
  Heal the sick and lead the blind.
  Just and holy is Thy name;
  I am all unrighteousness;
  Vile and full of sin I am,
  Thou art full of truth and grace.

No. 144. Refuge.

Leader:—I will lift up mine eyes un-to the hills from whence cometh my help. My help cometh from the Lord who made heaven and earth.

Response:—He shall be as an hiding place from the wind, and a covert from the tempest; as rivers of water in a dry place, as the shadow of a great rock in a weary land.

Leader:—Peace I leave with you, my peace I give unto you. Let not your heart be troubled, neither let it be afraid.

All Sing. 1st verse, No. 143. Jesus, lover, etc:

Leader:—Come unto me all ye that labor and are heavy laden and I will give you rest.

Response:—I will both lay me down

Refuge. Concluded.

in peace and sleep, for thou Lord only maketh me to dwell in safety.

Leader:—The Lord will be a refuge for the oppressed, a refuge in time of trouble.

Response:—What time I am afraid I will trust in thee.

All Sing. 2d verse, Other refuge have, etc.

Leader:—Behold he that keepeth Is-rael shall neither slumber nor sleep.

Response:—The name of the Lord is a strong tower. The righteous runneth into it, and is safe.

Leader:—Thou wilt keep him in per-fect peace whose mind is stayed on thee because he trusteth in thee.

All Sing: 3d verse, Thou, O Christ, etc.

No. 145. Jesus, I my Cross have Taken.

HENRY F. LYTE. ELLESIDE. 8. 7. D. (M. H. 643.) MOZART.

1. Je - sus, I my cross have tak-en, All to leave and fol-low thee;

Na - ked, poor, despised, for-sak-en, Thou from hence my all shalt be;

D. S.—Yet how rich is my con-di-tion, God and heav'n are still my own.

Per - ish ev - 'ry fond am-bi-tion, All I've sought, and hop'd, and known;

2 Let the world despise, forsake me,
They have left my Savior too;
Human hearts and looks deceive me,
Thou art not, like man, untrue;
And, while thou shalt smile upon me,
God of wisdom, love and might,
Foes may hate, and friends may shun
Show thy face and all is bright. [me,

3 Go, then, earthly fame and treasure!
Come, disaster, scorn and pain!
In thy service, pain is pleasure;
With thy favor, loss is gain:
I have called thee, "Abba, Father,"
I have stayed my heart on thee; [er,
Storms may howl, and clouds may gath-
All must work for good to me.

No. 146. Consecration.

Leader.—For the preaching of the cross is to them that perish, foolish-ness; but unto us which are saved it is the power of God.

Response.—Whosoever, therefore, shall confess me before men, him will I confess also before my Father which is in heaven.

Leader.—And he that taketh not his cross and followeth after me is not worthy of me.

All Sing. 1st verse, No. 145, Jesus, I my cross have taken, etc.

Leader.—And when he had called the people unto him, with his disciples also, he said unto them, Whosoever will come after me let him deny him-

Consecration. Concluded.

self and take up his cross and follow me.

Response.—And whosoever doth not bear his cross, and come after me, can not be my disciple.

Leader. For whosoever shall save his life shall lose it, but whosoever shall lose his life for my sake and the gospel's, the same shall save it.

All Sing. 2d verse, Let the world, etc.

Leader. For what shall it profit a man, if he gain the whole world and lose his own soul?

Response. Or what shall a man give in exchange for his soul?

All Sing. 3d verse, Go, then, earthly, etc.

No. 147. Bringing in the Sheaves.

From "SONGS OF GLORY." GEO. A. MINOR.

1. { Sow-ing in the morn-ing,sowing seeds of kindness,Sowing in the noon-tide
   { Waiting for the har-vest, and the time of reap-ing, (*Omit.*)

2 and the dewy eves; We shall come rejoicing,bringing in the sheaves.Bringing in the

Fine. CHORUS.

sheaves,bringing in the sheaves,We shall come re-joic-ing,bringing in the sheaves,

After Repeat D. S. to Fine.

2 Sowing in the sunshine, sowing in the shadows,
    Fearing neither clouds nor winter's chilling breeze;
    By and by the harvest, and the labor ended,
    We shall come rejoicing, bringing in the sheaves.

3 Go then, ever weeping, sowing for the Master,
    Though the loss sustained our spirit often grieves;
    When our weeping's over, he will bid us welcome,
    We shall come rejoicing, bringing in the sheaves.

No. 148. Bringing the Sheaves.

Leader.—Be not deceived; God is not mocked; for whatsoever a man soweth, that shall he also reap.

Response.—For he that soweth to his flesh, shall of the flesh reap corruption; but he that soweth to the Spirit shall of the Spirit reap life everlasting.

- *Leader.*—And the fruit of righteousness is sown in peace, of them that make peace.

All Sing: 1st verse No. 147, Sowing in the morning, etc.

Leader.—Say not ye, there are yet four months, and then cometh the harvest? behold I say unto you, lift up your eyes, and look on the fields; for they are white already to the harvest.

Bringing the Sheaves. Concluded.

Response.—And he that reapeth receiveth wages, and gathereth fruit unto life eternal, that both he that soweth and he that reapeth may rejoice together.

All Sing. 2d verse, Sowing in the sun-

Leader.—In the morning sow thy seed, and in the evening withold not thine hand: for thou knowest not whether shall prosper, either this or that, or whether they both shall be alike good.

Response.—He that goeth forth and weepeth, bearing precious seed, shall doubtless come again with rejoicing, bringing his sheaves with him.

All Sing. 3d verse, Go then, ever, etc.

No. 149. What a Friend.

H. BONAR.   8s, 7s, D.   C. C. CONVERSE.

1. What a friend we have in Je - sus, All our sins and griefs to bear!

Fine.

What a priv - i - lege to car - ry Ev - 'ry thing to God in pray'r!

D. S. *All be-cause we do not car - ry, Ev - 'ry thing to God in pray'r!*

D. S.

Oh, what peace we oft - en for - feit, Oh, what needless pain we bear,

2 Have we trials and temptations?
Is there trouble anywhere?
We should never be discouraged,
Take it to the Lord in prayer.
Can we find a friend so faithful,
Who will all our sorrows share?
Jesus knows our every weakness,
Take it to the Lord in prayer.

3 Are we weak and heavy laden,
Cumbered with a load of care,
Precious Savior, still our refuge,
Take it to the Lord in prayer.
Do thy friends despise, forsake thee?
Take it to the Lord in prayer,
In His arms He'll take and shield thee
Thou wilt find a solace there.

No. 150. Prayer.

Leader:—If my people, which are called by my name, shall humble themselves and pray, and seek my face, and turn from their wicked ways, then will I hear from heaven, and will forgive their sin.

Response:—And whatsoever ye shall ask in my name, that will I do, that the Father may be glorified in the Son.

All Sing: 1st verse, No. 149, What a, etc.

Leader;—In everything by prayer and supplication with thanksgiving let your requests be made known unto God.

Response:—The Spirit also helpeth our infirmities, for we know not what we should pray for as we ought; but the Spirit itself maketh intercession for us with groanings which cannot be uttered.

All Sing: 2d verse, Have we trials, etc.

Prayer. Concluded.

Leader:—Confess your faults one to another, and pray for one another, that ye may be healed. The effectual fervent prayer of a righteous man availeth much.

Response:—The sacrifice of the wicked is an abomination to the Lord; but the prayer of the upright is His delight.

All Sing: 3d verse, Are we weak, etc.

Leader:—After this manner therefore pray ye:

All:—Our Father which art in heaven, hallowed be thy name. Thy kingdom come. Thy will be done in earth as it is in heaven. Give us this day our daily bread. And forgive us our debts, as we forgive our debtors. And lead us not into temptation, but deliver us from evil. For thine is the kingdom, and the power, and the glory, forever, Amen.

No. 151. The Morning Light.

SAMUEL SMITH. WEBB. 7s, 6s. (M. II. 932.) GEO. WEBB.

1. { The morning light is breaking, The darkness disappears, }
   { The sons of earth are wak-ing; To pen-i- (Omit.) } ten-tial tears;

D. C.—Of na-tions in com-mo-tion, pre-pared for (Omit.) Zi-on's war.

Each breeze that sweeps the o-cean Brings ti-dings from a-far,

2 See heathen nations bending,
  Before the God of love,
  And thousand hearts ascending,
  In gratitude above;
  While sinners, now confessing,
  The gospel's call obey,
  And seek a Savior's blessing,
  A nation in a day.

3 Blest river of salvation,
  Pursue thy onward way:
  Flow thou to every nation,
  Nor in thy richness stay.
  Stay not till all the lowly,
  Triumphant reach their home;
  Stay not till all the holy
  Proclaim, "The Lord is come."

No. 152. Missionary. No. 2.

Leader.—In the beginning was the word, and the word was with God, and the word was God. The same was in the beginning with God. All things were made by him; and without him was not anything made that was made. In him was life; and the life was the light of men.

Response.—I am the light of the world; he that followeth me shall not walk in darkness, but shall have the light of life.

Leader.—This then is the message that we have heard of him, and declare unto you, that God is light, and in him is no darkness at all.

All Sing. 1st verse No. 151, The morning light is breaking, etc.

Leader.—The people that walked in darkness have seen a great light; they that dwell in the land of the shadow of death, upon them hath the light shined.

Missionary. Concluded.

Response.—Arise, shine; for thy light is come, and the glory of the Lord is risen upon thee.

Leader.—Look unto me, and be ye saved, all the ends of the earth; for I am God, and there is none else.

All Sing. 2d verse, See heathen nations bending, etc.

Leader.—And this gospel of the kingdom shall be preached in all the world for a witness unto all nations; and then shall the end come.

Response.—Go ye, therefore, and teach all nations, baptizing them in the name of the Father, and of the Son, and of the Holy Ghost: Teaching them to observe all things whatsoever I have commanded you; and, lo, I am with you alway, even unto the end of the world. Amen.

All Sing. 3d verse, Blest river of salvation, etc.

No. 153. Holy, Holy, Holy!

NICEA, 11, 12, 10.　　　Rev. JOHN B. DYKES.

1. Ho-ly, ho-ly, ho - ly! Lord God Al-might-y! Ear-ly in the
2. Ho-ly, ho-ly, ho - ly! All the saints adore Thee, Casting down their
3. Ho-ly, ho-ly, ho - ly! Tho' the darkness hide Thee, Tho' the eye of
4. Ho-ly, ho-ly, ho - ly! Lord God Almighty! All Thy works shall

morn-ing Our song shall rise to Thee; Ho - ly, ho - ly, ho - ly,
golden crowns A-round the glass-y sea; Cher - u -bim and Seraphim
sin-ful man Thy glo - ry may not see; On - ly Thou art ho - ly;
praise Thy name, In earth, and sky, and sea; Ho - ly, ho - ly, ho - ly.

Mer-ci-ful and Might-y! God in three Per-sons. Blessed Trin-i - ty!
Falling down be-fore Thee, Which wert, and art, and Ev-er-more shalt be.
There is none be-side Thee, Per - fect in power, in love, and pur-i - ty.
Mer-ci-ful and Might-y! God in three Per-sons, Blessed Trin-i - ty!

No. 154. Holy, Holy!

Holy, Holy! Concluded.

Leader:—Holy, holy, holy, is the Lord of hosts; the whole earth is full of His glory.

All sing: 1st verse, Holy, holy, holy! Lord, God Almighty! etc.

Leader:—For thou art not a God that hath pleasure in wickedness: neither shall evil dwell with Thee.

All sing: 2d verse, Holy, holy, holy! All the saints adore Thee, etc.

Leader:—Exalt the Lord, our God, and worship at His holy hill:- for the Lord, our God, is holy.

All sing: 3d verse, Holy, holy, holy! Lord, God Almighty! etc.

Leader:—The Lord is righteous in all His ways, and holy in all His works.

All sing: 4th verse, Holy, holy, holy! Lord, God Almighty! etc.

No. 155. How Gentle God's Commands.

PHILIP DODDRIDGE. DENNIS. S. M. GEO. NAEGELI.

1. How gen - tle God's commands! How kind His pre - cepts are!
2. Be - neath His watch-ful eye His saints se - cure - ly dwell;
3. Why should this anx - ious load Press down your wea - ry mind?
4. His good - ness stands approved, Unchang'd from day to day:

Come, cast your bur - dens on the Lord, And trust His constant care.
That hand which bears all na - ture up Shall guard His children well.
Haste to your heaven-ly Father's throne, And sweet re - fresh-ment find.
I'll drop my bur - den at His feet, And bear a song a - way.

No. 156. Wisdom.

Leader:—Remember now thy Creator in the days of thy youth. Serve him with gladness, and magnify his name forever!

Response:—What shall I render unto the Lord for all his benefits towards me? I will take the cup of salvation and call upon the name of the Lord.

Leader:—Give us, O Lord, the wisdom from above, which is first pure, then peaceable, gentle, easy to be entreated, full of mercy and good fruits, without partiality, and without hypocrisy.

Response:—Whence then cometh wisdom? and where is the place of understanding?

Leader:—Behold, the fear of the Lord, that is wisdom, and to depart from evil is understanding

Response:—Happy is the man that findeth wisdom, and the man that getteth understanding

Leader:—The merchandise of it is better than the merchandise of silver,

Wisdom. Concluded.

and the gain thereof than fine gold.

Response.—She is more precious than rubies.

Leader:—And all things thou canst desire are not to be compared unto her.

Response:—Length of days is in her right hand: and in her left hand riches and honor.

Leader:—Her ways are ways of pleasantness, and all her paths are peace.

Response:—She is a tree of life to them that lay hold upon her; and happy is every one that retaineth her.

Leader:—And beside this, giving all diligence, add to your knowledge temperance.

Response:—And to temperance, patience.

Leader:—And to patience, godliness.

Response:—And to godliness, brotherly kindness.

Leader:—And to brotherly kindness, charity.

All Sing: 1st and 2d verses, No. 155,
How gentle God's commands! etc.

PSALMS...

For Responsive or Concert Reading.

No. 157. PSALM 1.

1 Blessed *is* the man that walketh not in the counsel of the ungodly, nor standeth in the way of sinners, nor sitteth in the seat of the scornful.

2 But his delight *is* in the law of the Lord; and in His law doth he meditate day and night.

3 And he shall be like a tree planted by the rivers of water, that bringeth forth his fruit in his season; his leaf also shall not wither; and whatsoever he doeth shall prosper.

4 The ungodly *are* not so: but *are* like the chaff which the wind driveth away.

5 Therefore the ungodly shall not stand in the judgment, nor sinners in the congregation of the righteous.

6 For the Lord knoweth the way of the righteous: but the way of the ungodly shall perish.

No. 158. PSALM 8.

1 O Lord, our Lord, how excellent *is* Thy name in all the earth! who hast set Thy glory above the heavens.

2 Out of the mouth of babes and sucklings hast Thou ordained strength because of Thine enemies, That Thou mightest still the enemy and the avenger.

3 When I consider Thy heavens, the work of Thy fingers, the moon and the stars, which Thou hast ordained;

4 What is man, that Thou art mindful of him? and the son of man, that Thou visitest him?

5 For Thou hast made him a little lower than the angels, and hast crowned him with glory and honour.

6 Thou madest him to have dominion over the works of Thy hands; Thou hast put all *things* under his feet:

7 All sheep and oxen, yea, and the beasts of the field;

8 The fowl of the air, and the fish of the sea, *and* whatsoever passeth through the paths of the seas.

9 O Lord our Lord, how excellent *is* Thy name in all the earth!

No. 159. PSALM 15.

1 Lord, who shall abide in Thy tabernacle? who shall dwell in Thy holy hill?

2 He that walketh uprightly, and worketh righteousness, and speaketh the truth in his heart.

3 *He that* backbiteth not with his tongue, nor doeth evil to his neighbour, nor taketh up a reproach against his neighbour.

4 In whose eyes a vile person is contemned; but he honoureth them that fear the Lord. *He that* sweareth to *his own* hurt, and changeth not.

5 *He that* putteth not out his money to usury, nor taketh reward against the innocent. He that doeth these *things* shall never be moved.

No. 160. PSALM 17.

1 Hear the right, O Lord, attend unto my cry; give ear unto my prayer, *that goeth* not out of feigned lips.

2 Let my sentence come forth from Thy presence; let Thine eyes behold the things that are equal.

3 Thou hast proved mine heart; Thou hast visited *me* in the night; Thou hast tried me, *and* shalt find nothing: I am purposed *that* my mouth shall not transgress.

4 Concerning the works of men, by the word of Thy lips I have kept *me from* the paths of the destroyer.

5 Hold up my goings in Thy paths, *that* my footsteps slip not.

6 I have called upon Thee, for Thou wilt hear me, O God: incline Thine ear unto me, *and* hear my speech.

No. 161. PSALM 19.

1 The heavens declare the glory of God; and the firmament sheweth His handywork.

2 Day unto day uttereth speech, and night unto night sheweth knowledge.

3 *There* is no speech nor language, *where* their voice is not heard. *(over)*

4 Their line is gone out through all the earth, and their words to the end of the world. In them hath He set a tabernacle for the sun,

5 Which *is* as a bridegroom coming out of his chamber, *and* rejoiceth as a strong man to run a race.

6 His going forth *is* from the end of the heaven, and His circuit unto the ends of it: and there is nothing hid from the heat thereof.

7 The law of the Lord *is* perfect, converting the soul: the testimony of the Lord *is* sure, making wise the simple.

8 The statutes of the Lord *are* right, rejoicing the heart: the commandment of the Lord *is* pure, enlightening the eyes.

9 The fear of the Lord *is* clean, enduring for ever: the judgments of the Lord *are* true *and* righteous altogether.

10 More to be desired *are they* than gold, yea, than much fine gold: sweeter also than honey and the honeycomb.

11 Moreover by them is thy servant warned: *and* in keeping of them *there is* great reward.

12 Who can understand *his* errors? cleanse Thou me from secret *faults.*

13 Keep back Thy servant also from presumptuous *sins;* let them not have dominion over me: then shall I be upright, and I shall be innocent from the great transgression.

14 Let the words of my mouth, and the meditation of my heart, be acceptable in Thy sight, O Lord, my strength, and my Redeemer.

No. 162. PSALM 23.

1 The Lord is my Shepherd; I shall not want.

2 He maketh me to lie down in green pastures: He leadeth me beside the still waters.

3 He restoreth my soul: He leadeth me in the paths of righteousness for His name's sake.

4 Yea, though I walk through the valley of the shadow of death, I will fear no evil: for Thou *art* with me; Thy rod and Thy staff they comfort me.

5 Thou preparest a table before me in the presence of mine enemies: Thou anointest my head with oil; my cup runneth over.

6 Surely goodness and mercy shall follow me all the days of my life: and I will dwell in the house of the Lord for ever.

No. 163. PSALM 24.

1 The earth *is* the Lord's, and the fulness thereof; the world, and they that dwell therein.

2 For He hath founded it upon the seas, and established it upon the floods.

3 Who shall ascend into the hill of the Lord? or who shall stand in His holy place?

4 He that hath clean hands, and a pure heart; who hath not lifted up his soul unto vanity, nor sworn deceitfully.

5 He shall receive the blessing from the Lord, and righteousness from the God of his salvation.

6 This *is* the generation of them that seek Him, that seek thy face, O Jacob. Selah.

7 Lift up your heads, O ye gates; and be ye lifted up, ye everlasting doors; and the King of glory shall come in.

8 Who *is* the King of glory? The Lord, strong and mighty, the Lord mighty in battle.

9 Lift up your heads, O ye gates; even lift *them* up, ye everlasting doors; and the King of glory shall come in.

10 Who is this King of glory? The Lord of hosts, He *is* the King of glory. Selah.

No. 164. PSALM 27.

1 The Lord *is* my light and my salvation; whom shall I fear? the Lord *is* the strength of my life; of whom shall I be afraid?

2 When the wicked, *even* mine enemies and my foes, came upon me to eat up my flesh, they stumbled and fell.

3 Though a host should encamp against me, my heart shall not fear: though war should rise against me, in this *will* I *be* confident.

4 One *thing* have I desired of the Lord, that will I seek after; that I may dwell in the house of the Lord all the days of my life, to behold the beauty of the Lord, and to inquire in His temple.

5 For in the time of trouble He shall hide me in His pavilion: in the secret of His tabernacle shall He hide me;

He shall set me up upon a rock.

6 And now shall mine head be lifted up above mine enemies round about me: therefore will I offer in His tabernacle sacrifices of joy; I will sing, yea, I will sing praises unto the Lord.

7 Hear, O Lord, *when* I cry with my voice: have mercy also upon me, and answer me.

8 *When Thou saidst,* Seek ye my face; my heart said unto Thee, Thy face, Lord, will I seek.

9 Hide not Thy face *far* from me; put not Thy servant away in anger: Thou hast been my help; leave me not, neither forsake me, O God of my salvation.

10 When my father and my mother forsake me, then the Lord will take me up.

11 Teach me Thy way, O Lord; and lead me in a plain path, because of mine enemies.

12 Deliver me not over unto the will of mine enemies: for false witnesses are risen up against me, and such as breathe out cruelty.

13 *I had fainted,* unless I had believed to see the goodness of the Lord in the land of the living.

14 Wait on the Lord: be of good courage, and He shall strengthen thine heart: wait, I say, on the Lord.

No. 165. PSALM 32.

1 Blessed *is he whose* transgression *is* forgiven, *whose* sin *is* covered.

2 Blessed *is* the man unto whom the Lord imputeth not iniquity, and in whose spirit *there is* no guile.

3 When I kept silence, my bones waxed old through my roaring all the day long.

4 For day and night Thy hand was heavy upon me: my moisture is turned into the drought of summer. Selah.

5 I acknowledged my sin unto Thee, and mine iniquity have I not hid. I said, I will confess my transgressions unto the Lord; and Thou forgavest the iniquity of my sin. Selah.

6 For this shall every one that is godly pray unto Thee in a time when Thou mayest be found: surely in the floods of great waters they shall not come nigh unto him.

7 Thou *art* my hiding place; Thou shalt preserve me from trouble; Thou shalt compass me about with songs of deliverance. Selah.

8 I will instruct thee and teach thee in the way which thou shalt go: I will guide thee with mine eye.

9 Be ye not as the horse, *or* as the mule, *which* have no understanding: whose mouth must be held in with bit and bridle, lest they come near unto thee.

10 Many sorrows *shall be* to the wicked: but he that trusteth in the Lord, mercy shall compass him about.

11 Be glad in the Lord, and rejoice, ye righteous: and shout for joy, all *ye that are* upright in heart.

No. 166. PSALM 34.

1 I will bless the Lord at all times: His praise *shall* continually *be* in my mouth.

2 My soul shall make her boast in the Lord: the humble shall hear *thereof*, and be glad.

3 O magnify the Lord with me, and let us exalt His name together.

4 I sought the Lord, and He heard me, and delivered me from all my fears.

5 They looked unto Him, and were lightened: and their faces were not ashamed.

6 This poor man cried, and the Lord heard *him*, and saved him out of all his troubles.

7 The angel of the Lord encampeth round about them that fear Him, and delivereth them.

8 O taste and see that the Lord *is* good: blessed *is* the man *that* trusteth in Him.

9 O fear the Lord, ye His saints: for *there is* no want to them that fear Him.

10 The young lions do lack, and suffer hunger: but they that seek the Lord shall not want any good *thing*.

11 Come, ye children, hearken unto me: I will teach you the fear of the Lord.

12 What man *is he that* desireth life, *and* loveth *many* days, that he may see good?

13 Keep thy tongue from evil, and thy lips from speaking guile.

No. 167. PSALM 67.

1 God be merciful unto us, and bless us; *and* cause His face to shine upon us; Selah.

2 That Thy way may be known upon earth, Thy saving health among

(Over.)

all nations.

3 Let the people praise Thee, O God; let all the people praise Thee.

4 O let the nations be glad and sing for joy: for Thou shalt judge the people righteously, and govern the nations upon earth. Selah.

5 Let the people praise Thee, O God; let all the people praise Thee.

6 *Then* shall the earth yield her increase; *and* God, *even* our own God, shall bless us.

7 God shall bless us; and all the ends of the earth shall fear Him,

---

No. 168. PSALM 84.

1 How amiable *are* Thy tabernacles, O Lord of hosts!

2 My soul longeth, yea, even fainteth for the courts of the Lord: my heart and my flesh crieth out for the living God.

3 Yea, the sparrow hath found a house, and the swallow a nest for herself, where she may lay her young, *even* Thine altars, O Lord of hosts, my King, and my God.

4 Blessed *are* they that dwell in Thy house: they will be still praising Thee. Selah.

5 Blessed *is* the man whose strength *is* in Thee; in whose heart *are* the ways *of them.*

6 *Who* passing through the valley of Baca make it a well; the rain also filleth the pools.

7 They go from strength to strength, *every one of them* in Zion appeareth before God.

8 O Lord God of hosts, hear my prayer: give ear, O God of Jacob. Selah.

9 Behold, O God our shield, and look upon the face of Thine anointed.

10 For a day in Thy courts *is* better than a thousand. I had rather be a doorkeeper in the house of my God, than to dwell in the tents of wickedness.

11 For the Lord God *is* a sun and shield: the Lord will give grace and glory: no good *thing* will He withhold from them that walk uprightly.

12 O Lord of hosts, blessed *is* the man that trusteth in Thee.

No, 169. PSALM 91.

1 He that dwelleth in the secret place of the Most High shall abide un-

der the shadow of the Almighty.

2 I will say of the Lord, *He is* my refuge and my fortress: my God; in Him will I trust.

3 Surely He shall deliver thee from the snare of the fowler, *and* from the noisome pestilence.

4 He shall cover thee with His feathers, and under His wings shalt thou trust: His truth *shall be thy* shield and buckler.

5 Thou shalt not be afraid for the terror by night; *nor* for the arrow *that* flieth by day;

6 *Nor* for the pestilence *that* walketh in darkness; *nor* for the destruction *that* wasteth at noonday.

7 A thousand shall fall at thy side, and ten thousand at thy right hand; *but* it shall not come nigh thee.

8 Only with thine eyes shalt thou behold and see the reward of the wicked.

9 Because thou hast made the Lord, *which is* my refuge, *even* the Most High, thy habitation.

10 There shall no evil befall thee; neither shall any plague come nigh thy dwelling.

11 For He shall give His angels charge over thee, to keep thee in all thy ways.

12 They shall bear thee up in *their* hands, lest thou dash thy foot against a stone.

13 Thou shalt tread upon the lion and adder: the young lion and the dragon shalt thou trample under foot.

14 Because he hath set his love upon me, therefore will I deliver him: I will set him on high, because he hath known my name.

15 He shall call upon me, and I will answer him: I *will be* with him in trouble; I will deliver him, and honour him.

16 With long life will I satisfy him, and shew him my salvation.

No. 170. PSALM 93.

1 The Lord reigneth, He is clothed with majesty; the Lord is clothed with strength, *wherewith* He hath girded Himself: the world also is stablished, that cannot be moved.

2 Thy throne *is* established of old: Thou *art* from everlasting.

3 The floods have lifted up, O Lord, the floods have lifted up their voice; the floods lift up their waves,

4 The Lord on high *is* mightier than the noise of many waters, *yea, than* the mighty waves of the sea.

5 Thy testimonies are very sure: holiness becometh Thine house, O Lord, for ever.

No. 171. PSALM 95.

1 O come, let us sing unto the Lord; let us make a joyful noise to the Rock of our salvation.

2 Let us come before His presence with thanksgiving, and make a joyful noise unto Him with psalms.

3 For the Lord *is* a great God, and a great King above all gods.

4 In His hand *are* the deep places of the earth: the strength of the hills *is* His also.

5 The sea *is* His, and He made it: and His hands formed the dry *land*.

6 O come, let us worship and bow down: let us kneel before the Lord our Maker.

7 For He *is* our God; and we *are* the people of His pasture, and the sheep of His hand.

No, 172. PSALM 96.

1 O sing unto the Lord a new song: sing unto the Lord, all the earth.

2 Sing unto the Lord, bless His name; shew forth His salvation from day to day.

3 Declare His glory among the heathen, His wonders among all people.

4 For the Lord *is* great, and greatly to be praised. He *is* to be feared above all gods.

5 For all the gods of the nations *are* idols: but the Lord made the heavens.

6 Honour and majesty *are* before Him: strength and beauty *are* in His sanctuary.

7 Give unto the Lord, O ye kindreds of the people, give unto the Lord glory and strength.

8 Give unto the Lord the glory *due* unto His name: bring an offering, and come into His courts.

9 O worship the Lord in the beauty of holiness: fear before Him, all the earth.

10 Say among the heathen *that* the Lord reigneth: the world also shall be established that it shall not be moved: He shall judge the people righteously.

11 Let the heavens rejoice, and let the earth be glad; let the sea roar, and the fulness thereof.

12 Let the field be joyful, and all that *is* therein: then shall all the trees of the wood rejoice

13 Before the Lord: for He cometh, for He cometh to judge the earth: He shall judge the earth with righteousness, and the people with His truth.

No. 173. PSALM 98.

1 O sing unto the Lord a new song; for He hath done marvelous things: His right hand, and His holy arm, hath gotten Him the victory.

2 The Lord hath made known His salvation: His righteousness hath He openly shewed in the sight of the heathen.

3 He hath remembered His mercy and His truth toward the house of Israel: all the ends of the earth have seen the salvation of our God.

4 Make a joyful noise unto the Lord, all the earth: make a loud noise, and rejoice, and sing praise.

5 Sing unto the Lord with the harp; with the harp, and the voice of a psalm.

6 With trumpets and sound of cornet make a joyful noise before the Lord, the King.

7 Let the sea roar, and the fulness thereof; the world, and they that dwell therein.

8 Let the floods clap *their* hands: let the hills be joyful together

9 Before the Lord; for He cometh to judge the earth: with righteousness shall He judge the world, and the people with equity.

No. 174. PSALM 100,

1 Make a joyful noise unto the Lord, all ye lands.

2 Serve the Lord with gladness: come before His presence with singing.

3 Know ye that the Lord He *is* God: *it is* He *that* hath made us, and not we ourselves; *we are* His people and the sheep of His pasture.

4 Enter into His gates with thanksgiving, *and* into His courts with praise: be thankful unto Him, *and* bless His name.

5 For the Lord *is* good; His mercy *is* everlasting; and His truth *endureth* to all generations.

No. 175. PSALM 103.

1 Bless the Lord, O my soul: and all that is within me, *bless* His holy name.

2 Bless the Lord, O my soul, and forget not all His benefits.

3 Who forgiveth all thine iniquities; who healeth all thy diseases;

4 Who redeemeth thy life from destruction; who crowneth thee with lovingkindness and tender mercies;

5 Who satisfieth thy mouth with good *things; so that* thy youth is renewed like the eagle's.

6 The Lord executeth righteousness and judgment for all that are oppressed.

7 He made known His ways unto Moses, His acts unto the children of Israel.

8 The Lord *is* merciful and gracious, slow to anger, and plenteous in mercy,

9 He will not always chide: neither will He keep *His anger* for ever.

10 He hath not dealt with us after our sins; nor rewarded us according to our iniquities.

11 For as the heaven is high above the earth, *so* great is His mercy toward them that fear Him.

12 As far as the east is from the west, *so* far hath He removed our transgressions from us.

PART 2.

13 Like as a father pitieth *His* children, *so* the Lord pitieth them that fear Him.

14 For He knoweth our frame; He remembereth that we *are* dust.

15 *As for* man, his days *are* as grass: as a flower of the field, so he flourisheth.

16 For the wind passeth over it, and it is gone; and the place thereof shall know it no more.

17 But the mercy of the Lord *is* from everlasting to everlasting upon them that fear Him, and His righteousness unto children's children;

18 To such as keep His covenant, and to those that remember His commandments to do them.

19 The Lord hath prepared His throne in the heavens; and His kingdom ruleth over all.

20 Bless the Lord, ye His angels, that excel in strength, that do His commandments, hearkening unto the voice of His word,

21 Bless ye the Lord, all *ye* His hosts; *ye* ministers of His, that do His pleasure.

No. 176. PSALM 111.

1 Praise ye the Lord. I will praise the Lord with *my* whole heart, in the assembly of the upright, and *in* the congregation.

2 The works of the Lord *are* great, sought out of all them that have pleasure therein.

3 His work *is* honourable and glorious: and His righteousness endureth for ever.

4 He hath made His wonderful works to be remembered: the Lord *is* gracious and full of compassion.

5 He hath given meat unto them that fear Him: He will ever be mindful of His covenant.

6 He hath shewed His people the power of His works, that He may give them the heritage of the heathen.

7 The works of His hands *are* verity and judgment; all His commandments *are* sure.

8 They stand fast for ever and ever, *and are* done in truth and uprightness.

9 He sent redemption unto His people: He hath commanded His covenant for ever: holy and reverend *is* His name.

10 The fear of the Lord *is* the beginning of wisdom: a good understanding have all they that do *His commandments:* His praise endureth for ever.

No. 177. PSALM 112.

1 Praise ye the Lord. Blessed *is* the man *that* feareth the Lord, *that* delighteth greatly in His commandments.

2 His seed shall be mighty upon earth: the generation of the upright shall be blessed.

3 Wealth and riches *shall be* in His house: and His righteousness endureth for ever.

4 Unto the upright there ariseth light in the darkness: *He is* gracious, and full of compassion, and righteousness.

5 A good man sheweth favour, and lendeth: he will guide his affairs with discretion.

6 Surely he shall not be moved forever: the righteous shall be in everlasting remembrance,

7 He shall not be afraid of evil tidings: his heart is fixed, trusting in the Lord.

8 His heart is established, he shall not be afraid, until he see his desire upon his enemies.

9 He hath dispersed, he hath given to the poor; His righteousness endureth for ever; His horn shall be exalted with honour.

10 The wicked shall see it, and be grieved; he shall gnash with his teeth, and melt away: the desire of the wicked shall perish.

No. 178. PSALM 115.

1 Not unto us, O Lord, not unto us, but unto Thy name give glory, for Thy mercy, and for Thy truth's sake.

2 Wherefore should the heathen say, Where is now their God?

3 But our God is in the heavens: He hath done whatsoever He hath pleased.

4 Their idols are silver and gold, the work of men's hands.

5 They have mouths, but they speak not: eyes have they, but they see not.

6 They have ears, but they hear not: noses have they, but they smell not.

7 They have hands, but they handle not; feet have they, but they walk not: neither speak they through their throat.

8 They that make them are like unto them; so is every one that trusteth in them.

9 O Israel, trust thou in the Lord: He is their help and their shield.

10 O house of Aaron, trust in the Lord: He is their help and their shield.

11 Ye that fear the Lord, trust in the Lord: He is their help and their shield.

12 The Lord hath been mindful of us: He will bless us; He will bless the house of Israel; He will bless the house of Aaron.

13 He will bless them that fear the Lord, both small and great.

14 The Lord shall increase you more and more, you and your children.

15 Ye are blessed of the Lord which made heaven and earth.

16 The heaven, even the heavens are the Lord's: but the earth hath He given to the children of men.

17 The dead praise not the Lord, neither any that go down into silence.

18 But we will bless the Lord from this time forth and for ever more. Praise the Lord,

No. 179. PSALM 116.

1 I love the Lord, because He hath heard my voice and my supplications.

2 Because He hath inclined His ear unto me, therefore will I call upon Him as long as I live.

3 The sorrows of death compassed me, and the pains of hell gat hold upon me: I found trouble and sorrow.

4 Then called I upon the name of the Lord; O Lord, I beseech Thee, deliver my soul.

5 Gracious is the Lord, and righteous; yea, our God is merciful.

6 The Lord preserveth the simple: I was brought low, and He helped me.

7 Return unto thy rest, O my soul; for the Lord hath dealt bountifully with thee.

8 For Thou hast delivered my soul from death, mine eyes from tears, and my feet from falling.

9 I will walk before the Lord in the land of the living.

10 I believed, therefore have I spoken: I was greatly afflicted:

11 I said in my haste, All men are liars.

12 What shall I render unto the Lord for all His benefits toward me?

13 I will take the cup of salvation, and call upon the name of the Lord.

14 I will pay my vows unto the Lord now in the presence of all His people.

15 Precious in the sight of the Lord is the death of His saints.

16 O Lord, truly I am Thy servant; I am Thy servant, and the son of Thine handmaid: Thou hast loosed my bonds.

17 I will offer to Thee the sacrifice of thanksgiving, and will call upon the name of the Lord.

18 I will pay my vows unto the Lord now in the presence of all His people,

19 In the courts of the Lord's house, in the midst of thee, O Jerusalem. Praise ye the Lord.

No. 180. PSALM 118.

1 O Give thanks unto the Lord; for He is good: because His mercy endureth for ever.

2 Let Israel now say, that His mercy endureth for ever.

3 Let the house of Aaron now say, that His mercy endureth for ever.

4 Let them now that fear the Lord say, that His mercy endureth for ever.

5 I called upon the Lord in distress: th: Lord answered me, *and set me* in a large place.

6 The Lord *is* on my side, I will not fear: what can man do unto me?

7 The Lord taketh my path with them that help me: therefore shall I see *my desire* upon them that hate me.

8 *It is* better to trust in the Lord than to put confidence in man.

9 *It is* better to trust in the Lord than to put confidence in princes.

10 All nations compass me about: but in the name of the Lord will I destroy them.

11 They compassed me about; yea, they compassed me about: but in the name of the Lord I will destroy them.

12 They compassed me about like bees: they are quenched as the fire of thorns: for in the name of the Lord I will destroy them.

13 Thou hast thrust sore at me that I might fall: but the Lord helped me.

14 The Lord *is* my strength and song, and is become my salvation.

PART 2.

15 The voice of rejoicing and salvation *is* in the tabernacles of the righteous: the right hand of the Lord doeth valiantly.

16 The right hand of the Lord is exalted: the right hand of the Lord doeth valiantly.

17 I shall not die, but live, and declare the works of the Lord.

18 The Lord hath chastened me sore: but He hath not given me over unto death.

19 Open to me the gates of righteousness: I will go into them, *and* I will praise the Lord:

20 This gate of the Lord, into which the righteous shall enter.

21 I will praise Thee: for Thou hast heard me, and art become my salvation.

22 The stone *which* the builders refused is become the head *stone* of the corner.

23 This is the Lord's doing; it *is* marvelous in our eyes.

24 This *is* the day *which* the Lord hath made; we will rejoice and be glad in it.

25 Save now, I beseech Thee, O Lord: O Lord, I beseech Thee, send now prosperity.

26 Blessed *be* he that cometh in the name of the Lord: we have blessed you out of the house of the Lord.

27 God *is* the Lord, which hath shewed us light: bind the sacrifice with cords, *even* unto the horns of the altar.

28 Thou *art* my God, and I will praise Thee: *Thou art* my God, I will exalt Thee.

29 O give thanks unto the Lord; for *He is* good: for His mercy *endureth* for ever.

No. 181. PSALM 119.

ALEPH.

1 Blessed *are* the undefiled in the way, who walk in the law of the Lord.

2 Blessed *are* they that keep His testimonies, *and that* seek Him with the whole heart.

3 They also do no iniquity: they walk in His ways.

4 Thou hast commanded *us* to keep thy precepts diligently.

5 O that my ways were directed to keep Thy statutes!

6 Then shall I not be ashamed, when I have respect unto all Thy commandments.

7 I will praise Thee with uprightness of heart, when I shall have learned Thy righteous judgments.

8 I will keep Thy statutes: O forsake me not utterly.

No. 182. PSALM 121.

1 I will lift up mine eyes unto the hills, from whence cometh my help.

2 My help *cometh* from the Lord, which made heaven and earth.

3 He will not suffer thy foot to be moved: He that keepeth thee will not slumber.

4 Behold, He that keepeth Israel shall neither slumber nor sleep.

5 The Lord *is* thy keeper: the Lord *is* thy shade upon thy right hand.

6 The sun shall not smite thee by day, nor the moon by night.

7 The Lord shall preserve thee from all evil: He shall preserve thy soul.

8 The Lord shall preserve thy going out and thy coming in from this time forth, and even for evermore.

No. 183. PSALM 122,

1 I was glad when they said unto me, Let us go into the house of the Lord.

2 Our feet shall stand within thy

(*Over.*)

gates, O Jerusalem.

3 Jerusalem is builded as a city that is compact together:

4 Whither the tribes go up, the tribes of the Lord, unto the testimony of Israel, to give thanks unto the name of the Lord.

5 For there are set thrones of judgment, the thrones of the house of David.

6 Pray for the peace of Jerusalem: they shall prosper that love Thee.

7 Peace be within thy walls, and prosperity within thy palaces.

8 For my brethren and companions' sakes, I will now say, Peace be within thee.

9 Because of the house of the Lord our God I will seek thy good.

No. 184. PSALM 125.

1 They that trust in the Lord shall be as mount Zion, which cannot be removed, but abideth for ever.

2 As the mountains are round about Jerusalem, so the Lord is round about His people from henceforth even for ever.

3 For the rod of the wicked shall not rest upon the lot of the righteous; lest the righteous put forth their hands unto iniquity.

4 Do good, O Lord, unto those that be good, and to them that are upright in their hearts.

5 As for such as turn aside unto their crooked ways, the Lord shall lead them forth with the workers of iniquity: but peace shall be upon Israel.

No. 185.   Lord, Have Mercy.

M. C. F.

Lord, have mercy upon us and in-cline our hearts to keep Thy law.   A - men.

No. 186.   The Ten Commandments.

And God spake all these words, saying:

I. Thou shalt have no other Gods before me.

Sing. Lord, Have Mercy, etc.

II. Thou shalt not make unto thee any graven image, or any likeness of any thing that is in heaven above, or that is in the earth beneath, or that is in the water under the earth: thou shalt not bow down thyself to them: nor serve them; for I the Lord thy God am a jealous God, visiting the iniquity of the fathers upon the children unto the third and fourth generation of them that hate me; and showing mercy unto thousands of them that love me, and keep my commandments.

Sing. Lord, Have Mercy, etc.

III. Thou shalt not take the name of the Lord thy God in vain: for the Lord will not hold him guiltless that taketh His name in vain.

IV. Remember the Sabbath-day, to keep it holy. Six days shalt thou labor, and do all thy work: but the seventh day is the Sabbath of the Lord thy God: in it thou shalt not do any work: thou, nor thy son, nor thy daughter, thy man-servant, nor thy maid-servant, nor thy cattle, nor thy stranger that is within thy gates: for in six days the Lord made heaven and earth, the sea, and all that in them is, and rested the seventh day: wherefore the Lord blessed the Sabbath-day, and hallowed it.

Sing. Lord, Have Mercy, etc.

V. Honor thy father and thy mother: that thy days may be long upon the land which the Lord thy God giveth thee.

VI. Thou shalt not kill.

VII. Thou shalt not commit adultery.

VIII. Thou shalt not steal.

IX. Thou shalt not bear false witness against thy neighbor.

X. Thou shalt not covet thy neighbor's house, thou shalt not covet thy neighbor's wife, nor his man-servant, nor his maid-servant, nor his ox, nor his ass, nor anything that is thy neighbor's.

Sing. Lord, Have Mercy, etc.

No. 187. Consecration Service.

Leader. Have mercy upon me, O God, according to thy loving-kindness: according unto the multitude of thy tender mercies blot out my transgressions.

Response. Wash me thoroughly from mine iniquity, and cleanse me from my sin.

L. For I acknowledge my transgression: and my sin is ever before me.

R. Behold, thou desirest truth in the inward parts: and in the hidden part thou shalt make me to know wisdom.

L. Purge me with hyssop, and I shall be clean: wash me, and I shall be whiter than snow.

R. Make me to hear joy and gladness; that the bones which thou hast broken may rejoice.

L. Hide thy face from my sins, and blot out all mine iniquities.

R. Create in me a clean heart, O God; and renew a right spirit within me.

L. Cast me not away from thy presence; and take not thy Holy Spirit from me.

R. Restore unto me the joy of thy salvation, and uphold me with thy free Spirit.

All. Then will I teach transgressors thy ways, and sinners shall be converted unto thee.

All kneeling, repeat together:

"I renounce the devil and all his works, the vain pomp and glory of the world, with all covetous desires of the same, and the carnal desires of the flesh, so that I will not follow nor be led by them. . . . Having been baptized in this faith, I will obediently keep God's holy will and commandments and walk in the same all the days of my life, God being my helper."

Prayer by the pastor.

Kneeling, sing Hymn No. 67.

No. 188. Consecration Service.

Leader. Therefore if any man be in Christ, he is a new creature; old things are passed away; behold, all things are become new.

Response. And all things are of God, who hath reconciled us to himself by Jesus Christ, and hath given to us the ministry of reconciliation.

L. To wit, that God was in Christ reconciling the world unto himself, not imputing their trespasses unto them; and hath committed unto us the word of reconciliation.

R. Now then we are embassadors for Christ, as though God did beseech you by us; we pray you in Christ's stead, be ye reconciled to God.

L. For he hath made him to be sin for us, who knew no sin; that we might be made the righteousness of God in him.

R. Now, concerning spiritual gifts, brethren, I would not have you ignorant.

L. Ye knew that ye were Gentiles, carried away unto these dumb idols, even as ye were led.

All kneeling, repeat together.

* "And this day, do I, O Lord, with the utmost solemnity and sincerity, surrender myself to thee, desiring nothing so much as to be wholly thine. I renounce all former lords that have had dominion over me, and I consecrate to thee all that I am and have; the faculties of my mind, the members of my body, my worldly possessions, my time, my influence with others, to be all used entirely for thy glory, and resolutely employed in obedience to thy commands as long as thou shalt continue my life. . . To thee I leave the management of all events, and say without reserve, '*Thy will be done.*' "

Kneeling, sing Hymn No. 92,

No. 189.   Benediction.

Leader. The Lord bless thee and keep thee.
Response. The Lord make his face shine upon thee, and be gracious unto thee.
All. The Lord lift up his countenance upon thee, and give thee peace. Amen.

No. 190. Opening Service
For Young People's Meetings.

Leader. It is good to sing praises unto our God; for it is pleasant; and praise is comely.

Congregation. O come, let us sing unto the Lord:

L. Let us make a joyful noise to the Rock of our salvation.

C. Praise ye the Lord from the heavens; praise him in the heights.

L. Both young men, and maidens; old men, and children:

C. Let them praise the name of the Lord.

L. How amiable are thy tabernacles, O Lord of hosts!

C. I had rather be a doorkeeper in the house of my God, than to dwell in the tents of wickedness.

L. Out of Zion, the perfection of beauty, God hath shined.

C. Christ also loved the church, and gave himself for it;

L. That he might sanctify and cleanse it with the washing of water by the word.

C. That he might present it to himself a glorious church, not having spot, or wrinkle, or any such thing; but that it should be holy and without blemish.

L. One thing have I desired of the Lord, that I will seek after.

C. That I may dwell in the house of the Lord all the days of my life, to behold the beauty of the Lord and to inquire in his temple.

Singing. Jesus, Savior, Pilot Me. No. 103.

Prayer.

No. 191. Opening Service
For the Sunday-School.

Leader. O worship the Lord in the beauty of holiness.

School. Let the whole earth stand in awe of him.

L. The law of the Lord is perfect, converting the soul.

S. The testimony of the Lord is sure, making wise the simple.

L. The statutes of the Lord are right, rejoicing the heart: the commandment of the Lord is pure, enlightening the eyes.

S. The fear of the Lord is clean, enduring forever: the judgments of the Lord are true and righteous altogether.

L. More to be desired are they than gold, yea, than much fine gold:

S. Sweeter also than honey and the honey-comb.

L. Moreover by them is thy servant warned;

S. And in keeping of them there is great reward.

All. Let the words of my mouth, and the meditation of my heart, be acceptable in thy sight, O Lord, my strength, and my redeemer.

Singing. Love Divine, No. 104.

Prayer.

No. 192. The Apostles' Creed.

I believe in God the Father Almighty, Maker of heaven and earth; and in Jesus Christ his only Son our Lord; who was conceived by the Holy Ghost, born of the Virgin Mary, suffered under Pontius Pilate; was crucified, dead and buried; the third day he rose from the dead; he ascended into heaven, and sitteth on the right hand of God the Father Almighty; from thence He shall come to judge the quick and the dead.

I believe in the Holy Ghost; the Holy Catholic Church, the communion of saints; the forgiveness of sins; the resurrection of the body, and the life everlasting. Amen.

Having been baptized in this faith, I will obediently keep God's holy will and commandments, and walk in the same all the days of my life, God being my helper.

No. 193.   Benediction,

Now the God of peace, that brought again from the dead our Lord Jesus, that great Shepherd of the sheep, through the blood of the everlasting covenant, make you perfect in every good work, to do His will, working in you that which is wellpleasing in His sight, through Jesus Christ; to whom be glory for ever and ever. Amen.

No. 194.   Benediction,

The grace of our Lord Jesus Christ be with you all. Amen.

No. 195. That Old, Old Story is True.

D B. WATKINS.

E. O. EXCELL.

1. There's a won-der-ful sto-ry I've heard long a-go, 'Tis
2. They told of a be-ing so love-ly and pure, That
3. He a-rose and as-cend-ed to heav-en, we're told, Tri-
4. Oh, that won-der-ful sto-ry I love to re-peat, Of

call'd "The sweet sto-ry of old" I hear it so oft-en, wher-
came to the earth to dwell, To seek for His lost ones, and
umph-ant o'er death and hell; He's pre-par-ing a place in that
peace and good will to men; There's no sto-ry to me that is

ev-er I go, That same old sto-ry was told; And I've
make them se-cure From death and the pow-er of hell; That
cit-ty of gold, Where lov'd ones for-ev-er may dwell. Where our
half so sweet, As I hear it a-gain and a-gain. He in-

thought it was strange that so oft-en they'd tell That sto-ry as
He was despis'd and with thorns He was crown'd, On the cross was ex-
kin-dred we'll meet, and we'll nev-er more part, And oh, while I
vites you to come—He will free-ly re-ceive, And this message He

That Old, Old Story is True. Concluded.

if it were new; But I've found out the rea-son they loved it so
tend-ed to view; But Oh, what sweet peace in my heart since I've
tell it to you, It is peace to my soul, it is joy to my
send-eth to you, "There's a man-sion in glo-ry for all who be-

REFRAIN.

well, That old, old sto-ry is true. That old, old sto-ry is true,
found That old, old sto-ry is true. That old, old sto-ry is true,
heart, That old, old sto-ry is true. That old, old sto-ry is true,
lieve," That old, old sto-ry is true. That old, old sto-ry is true,

It is true,

That old, old sto-ry is true; But I've found out the rea-son they
That old, old sto-ry is true; But Oh, what sweet peace in my
That old, old sto-ry is true; It is peace to my soul, it is
That old, old sto-ry is true; "There's a man-sion in glo-ry for

It is true;

loved it so well, That old, old sto-ry is true.
heart since I've found That old, old sto-ry is true.
joy to my heart. That old, old sto-ry is true.
all who be-lieve," That old, old sto-ry is true.

No. 196. To the Harvest Field.

COPYRIGHT, 1898, BY E. O. EXCELL.
WORDS AND MUSIC.

C. H. G.

CHAS. H GABRIEL.

1. A band of faith-ful reap-ers we, Who gath-er for e - ter - ni -
2. We are a faith-ful gleaning band, And la - bor at our Lord's com-
3. The golden hours like moments fly, And harvest days are pass-ing

ty,   The gold - en sheaves of rip - ened grain From ev - 'ry
mand, Un-yield-ing, loy - al, tried and true, For lo! the
by;   Then take thy rust - y sick - le down, And la - bor

val - ley, hill and plain; Our song is one the reap - ers
reap - ers are but few; Be-hold the wav - ing har - vest
for a fade - less crown; Why will you id - ly stand and

sing, In hon - or of their Lord and King— The Mas - ter
field A - bun-dant with a gold - en yield; And hear the
wait? Be-hold, the hour is grow-ing late! Can you to

To the Harvest Field. Concluded.

of the har - vest wide, Who for a world of sin-ners died.
Lord of har - vest say To all: "Go reap for me to - day."
judgment bring but leaves, While here are waiting golden sheaves?

CHORUS.

To the har - vest field a - way, For the Mas - ter

call - eth; There is work for all to-day. Ere the dark-ness

fell - eth. Swift - ly do the moments fly, Har-vest days are

go - ing by, Going, go-ing, go-ing, go-ing by.

No. 197. Why Stand Ye Here Idle?

J. L. McDONALD.   COPYRIGHT, 1892, BY E. O. EXCELL.   E. O. EXCELL.

DUET. SOP. AND TENOR.

1. Why stand ye here i-dle? there's la-bor for all, The vine-yard needs
2. Why stand ye here i-dle? a broth-er's in need, His cries as-cend
3. Why stand ye here i-dle? a soul's be-ing lost, Speak, speak words of
4. Why stand ye here i-dle? O la-bor each day, To lead men to
5. Why stand ye here i-dle? a harp and a crown Are wait-ing in

workmen, the weeds are grown tall, The ripe fruit is wast-ing for
heav'nward, then pray you, give heed; For food and for raiment he
warn-ing, what-ev-er the cost; The soul you may res-cue from
Je-sus, the Truth, Life and Way; The Spir-it has prom-ised its
glo-ry for sons of re-nown Who la-bor and suf-fer for

lack of strong hands, "Why stand ye here i-dle?" The Mas-ter de-mands.
suf-fers to-night, Then ren-der as-sist-ance; O dare to do right.
sin and from shame, And give to the Sav-ior to praise His dear name.
presence to lend, To com-fort and strengthen, till la-bors shall end.
tru-est and best, Then la-bor and en-ter the ha-ven of rest.

CHORUS.

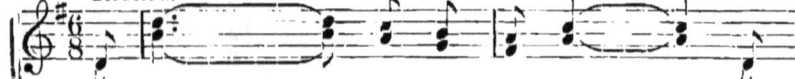

Oh, why . . . . . . stand ye i-dle . . . . . Oh,
Oh, why stand ye i-dle, so i-dle all day? Oh,

Why Stand Ye Here Idle? Concluded.

why . . . stand ye   i - dle . . . .   Oh, why . . . . . stand ye
why stand ye i - dle, so   i - dle all day?   Oh,   why stand ye   i - dle, so

i - dle, . . .   i - - dle all   day? . . . . .   The
i - dle all   day,   i - dle all   day,   i - dle all day? The

har - - vest is pass - ing, . . .   The   har - -
har-vest   is [pass - ing, is   pass - ing a - way,   The   har - vest   is

- vest   is   pass - ing, . . .   The   har - - vest is
pass - ing,   is   pass - ing a - way,   The   har - vest   is pass - ing, is

pass - ing, . . .   pass - - ing a - way . . . . .
pass - ing   a - way,   pass - ing   a - way,   pass-ing   a - way.

No. 198. Marching, Marching.

COPYRIGHT, 1898, BY E. O. EXCELL.
WORDS AND MUSIC.

C. H. G.

CHAS. H. GABRIEL.

1. Beau-ti-ful songs we sing un-to our Sav-ior King, Spreading the
2. Telling His wond'rous love, pointing to things a-bove, Scat-ter-ing
3. Seeking the lambs a-stray out on the broad high-way, Tell-ing a-

joys of His won-der-ful sal-va-tion; Je-sus, the
sun-light up-on a world of sad-ness; Do-ing a
gain and a-gain the won-d'rous sto-ry, How in a

Cru-ci-fied,—He is our Friend and Guide, And with Him we
kind-ly deed, sow-ing the pre-cious seed, That will yield, at
low-ly stall, He, for the sins of all, Slept,—the King, Re-

can-not go a-stray. Try-ing to do His will, and His com-
last an hun-dred fold; Lift-ing a brother's load, pointing him
deemer, Prince of Peace, Is a di-vine em-ploy,—is a de-

mands ful-fill, Un-to His name we will sing with ex-ul-
in the road, Cheering him on-ward with words of joy and
light, a joy, Fill-ing the heart with His love, the soul with

Marching, Marching. Concluded.

ta - tion; Proud-ly floats our ban - ner o'er us, vic - t'ry
glad - ness, Fills the heart with peace and pleas-ure vain words
glo - ry! Now in ev - 'ry land and na - tion of the

lies before us; Je - sus lead-ing, hap - py is the way!
can-not meas-ure, And a hap - pi-ness that is un - told.
whole cre - a - tion Let His praise begin, and nev - er cease.

CHORUS.

Gai - ly sing - ing, our voic - es ring - ing, We are a -
Mu - sic swell - ing, the sto - ry tell - ing, We'll make the

hap-py, hap-py band of vol - un-teers, Marching, marching,
ev - er-last-ing arches ring with cheers, (*Omit.*)

up the nar-row way; Marching, marching, onward day by day.

No. 199.   That Beautiful Stream.

E. TORBEY.   COPYRIGHT, 1889, BY E. O. EXCELL.   E. O EXCELL.

1. I'll sing of a stream,......... of a beau-ti-ful stream,...........
2. I'll sing of a stream,......... of a beau-ti-ful stream,...........
3. I'll sing of a stream, ... of a beau-ti-ful stream,...........
4. I'll sing of a stream,......... of a beau-ti-ful stream,...........

1. I'll sing of a stream,   of a beautiful stream,
2. I'll sing of a stream,   of a beautiful stream,
3. I'll sing of a stream,   of a beautiful stream,
4. I'll sing of a stream,   of a beautiful stream,

'Tis flowing to-day............... thro' the sweet Canaan Land...............
Which gladdens the hearts........... ... in the cit-y of God...............
That fountain of God,............... which was opened for sin,.................
That fountain that now............ .... and for-ev-er is free.................

'Tis flowing to - day   thro' the sweet Canaan Land,
Which gladdens the hearts   in the cit - y of God,
That fountain of God,   which was opened for sin,
That fountain that now   and for-ev-er is free,

Its waters gleam bright............ in their heavenly light..............,
It flows from a - bove.............. thro' God's infinite love ....
That stream from His side... .... who for sinners once died, ...
I'll sing of that flood .... which is crimsoned with blood.......

Its waters gleam bright   in their heavenly light,
It flows from above   thro' God's infinite love,
That stream from His side   who for sinners once died,
I'll sing of that flood   which is crimsoned with blood

That Beautiful Stream. Concluded.

And spark - les o'er sil-ver - y sand. Go wash,
And spreads its sweet waters abroad. Go wash,
He's healed who but plunges within. Go wash, CHORUS.
From sin, it has cleansed even me. Go wash, Go wash in that

And sparkles, sparkles o'er sil - ver - y sand. Go wash,
And spreads its wa-ters, sweet wa-ters a - broad. Go wash, Go wash, go wash in that
He's healed who plunges, who plunges with - in. Go wash,
From sin, from sin it has cleansed ev-en me. Go wash,

beau-ti-ful stream,.................. Go wash...... in that beautiful

beau-ti-ful stream, in that beautiful stream, Go wash, go wash in that beau-ti-ful

stream,..................... Go wash.......... in that beau-ti-ful

stream, in that beau - ti - ful stream, Go wash, go wash in that beau-ti - ful

stream............... .... 'Tis flowing at the cross for you.

stream, in that beau - ti - ful stream, 'Tis flow-ing at the cross for you.

No. 200.   Rock of Ages.

A. M. TOPLADY.   COPYRIGHT, 1884, BY E. O. EXCELL.   E. O. EXCELL.

1. Rock   of   A - - ges   cleft   for   me,
2. Could   my   tears   for - ev - - er   flow,
3. While   I   draw   this fleet - - ing breath,

1. Rock of A - ges, cleft for me,   Blest Rock of A - ges, cleft for me,
2. Could my tears for - ev - er flow,   Oh! Could my tears for - ev - er flow,
3. While I draw this fleet-ing breath, Yes, While I draw   this fleet-ing breath,

Let   me   hide   my - self   in   thee;
Could my   zeal   no   lan - - guor know,
When   mine   eyes   shall close   in   death,

Let me hide my - self in thee,   Oh! Let me hide   my - self in thee;
Could my zeal no   lan-guor know, Oh! Could my zeal   no   languor know,
When mine eyes shall close in death, Yes, When mine eyes shall close in death,

Let   the   wa - - ter and   the blood,
These for   sin   could not   a - tone,
When   I   rise   to worlds   un - known,

Let the wa - ter and the blood, Oh! Let the wa - ter and the blood,
These for sin could not a - tone, No, These for sin   could not a - tone,
When I rise   to worlds un-known, Yes, When I rise   to worlds un-known

Rock of Ages. Concluded.

From thy wound - ed side which flow'd,
Thou must save and thou a - lone,
And be - hold thee on thy throne;

From thy wound - ed side which flow'd, Yes, From thy wound-ed side which flow'd,
Thou must save and thou a - lone, Yes, Thou must save and thou a - lone,
And be - hold thee on thy throne, Yes, And be-hold thee on thy throne,

Be of sin the dou - - ble cure,
In my hand no price I bring;
Rock of A - - ges, cleft for me,

rit.

Be of sin the dou - ble cure, Yes, Be of sin the dou-ble cure,
In my hand no price I bring, Lord, In my hand no price I bring,
Rock of A - ges, cleft for me, Blest Rock of A - ges, cleft for me,

Save from wrath and make me pure.
Sim - ·ply to thy cross I cling.
Let me hide my - self in thee.

Repeat pp.

Save from wrath and make me pure, Yes, Save from wrath and make me pure.
Sim - ply to thy cross I cling, Lord, Sim-ply to thy cross I cling.
Let me hide my - self in thee, Oh, Let me hide my - self in thee.

No. 201. Red, White and Blue.

Maestoso.

1. O Co-lum-bia! the gem of the o-cean, The home of the
2. When war winged its wide des-o-la-tion, And threatened the
3. The Un-ion, the Un-ion for-ev-er, Our glo-ri-ous

brave and the free, The shrine of each pat-riot's de-vo-tion, A
land to de-form, The ark then of freedom's foundation, Co-
na-tion's sweet hymn, May the wreaths it has won never wither, Nor the

world of-fers hom-age to thee. Thy man-dates make he-roes as-
-lum-bia, rode safe thro' the storm; With her garlands of vic-t'ry a-
star of its glo-ry grow dim, May the ser-vice u-ni-ted ne'er

Red, White and Blue. Concluded.

sem-ble, When Lib-er-ty's form stands in view, Thy banners make tyr-
-round her, When so proudly she bore her brave crew, With her flag proudly float-
sev - er, But they to their col-ors prove true! The Ar - my and Na-

FINE.

- an -ny trem-ble, When borne by the red, white and blue.
- ing be - fore her, The boast of the red, white and blue.
- vy for ev - er, Three cheers for the red, white and blue.

FULL CHORUS.

When borne by the red, white and blue, When borne by the
The boast of the red, white and blue, The boast of the
Three cheers for the red, white and blue, Three cheers for the

D. S.

red, white and blue, Thy ban-ners make tyr - an - ny
red, white and blue, With her flag proudly float-ing be-
red, white and blue, The Ar - my and Na - vy for-

No. 202.   Doxology.

THOS. KEN.   OLD HUNDRED. L. M.   G. FRANC.

Praise God from whom all blessings flow; Praise Him, all creatures here below;

Praise Him a-bove ye heav'nly host, Praise Father, Son and Ho-ly Ghost.

No. 203.   Invitation to Worship.

(See music above.)

1 All people that on earth do dwell,
Sing to the Lord with cheerful voice:
Him serve with fear, His praise forth tell
Come ye before Him, and rejoice.

2 The Lord, ye know, is God indeed,
Without our aid He did us make;
We are His flock, He doth us feed,
And for His sheep He doth us take.

3 O enter then His gates with praise,
Approach with joy His courts unto:
Praise, laud, and bless His name always
For it is seemly so to do.

4 For why? the Lord our God is good.
His mercy is forever sure;
His truth at all times firmly stood,
And shall from age to age endure.

WILLIAM KETHE.

No. 204.   Doxology.

THOS. KEN.   SESSIONS. L. M.   L. O. EMERSON.

1. All people that on earth do dwell, Sing to the Lord with cheerful voice:

Him serve with fear, His praise forth tell, Come ye before Him and re-joice.

No. 205.   Gloria Patri.

1. Glory be to the Father, and to the Son,   and   to the Ho-ly Ghost;
2. As it was in the beginning,
    is now, and ev-er shall be, world without end, A-men.

INDEX.

Titles in SMALL CAPS—First Lines in Roman.

155

INDEX.

INDEX.

INDEX.

Topical Index.

159

TOPICAL INDEX.

Metrical Index.